Pipe Dream

Chasing A Man's Job

Jennie Jones

Pipe Dream. Chasing a Man's Job

by Jennie Jones

Published in 2024 by Away With The Angels Publishing.

A CIP catalogue record for this title is available from the British Library.

ISBN 978-1-0686794-0-7

Contents

Foreword

What kind of animal am I?

What kind of animal am I? My husband looks me up and down. He's just come home from work. He's a telecoms engineer, and he's spent the day climbing telegraph poles and fixing phone lines in the winter rain. He looks puzzled.

"You're doing woman things," he says.

I'm wearing a green flowery apron, and I am cradling a big pink bowl of ingredients for banana bread. I can't remember the last time I did some baking, so no wonder he looks surprised.

Yesterday he also looked me up and down, also in the kitchen, and looked bemused.

My car had sprung an oil leak from the engine gasket. As part of the repair, I'd brought the gasket cover into the house for cleaning. He'd come into the kitchen to start preparing the evening meal — roast pork, with all the trimmings. He is an excellent cook, which is why he prepares most of our meals.

"It's a gender reversal," he'd said. "Not many men walk into their kitchens to find their women cleaning car parts."

But then, as we've already agreed, I'm not a 'normal' woman. Whatever normal might be. My husband — his name is Rob — is proud to live with a woman who owns an angle grinder. He likes to recount the day he went to work, when I ripped out the bath and smashed the tiles off the bathroom wall. He came home to find the toilet in the spare room.

You'd think I'd done it without warning, the way he tells the story. We did discuss it first. But the story sounds better the way he tells it.

"Just don't use the loo," I'd said, as though he would have. "It's not plumbed in."

He's also proud of the time I ripped his back-boiler out (which had sat in the corner of his living room.) It needed to come out. I installed a new, modern boiler, in the kitchen.

Rob is proud of me for all these things. I should be proud of myself too. For the things I've achieved are unusual for a woman. Statistics show that only 1 percent of plumbers in the UK is female. I'm one of them. I'm also a Gas Safe registered engineer — of which an estimated one in 250 is female. *1

I've come a long way since I enrolled on an apprenticeship course in plumbing at my local college, 15 years earlier. I tend to forget where I've come from. I focus too much on what I don't know, and expect so much of myself.

I expect myself to match the guys who have been out there for 30 plus years. I forget that one day, they too were beginners, looking at a mountain of information and skills to master.

As I start to write this book, at the beginning of the third Covid lockdown, in early 2021, I can see my plumbing van from my kitchen window. It's a small, white 2004 Berlingo. I've fitted a pipe carrier to the roof-rack, which I've painted baby pink (they were only sold in white or chrome). The front seat covers are hot pink. The back, glass windows have grilles across them. But for extra security, I've fitted a set of brown curtains across them, which I pull shut when I'm not in the van. They look like campervan curtains.

The van is named Betty, as in Betty The Berlingo. It lives on the hard standing behind our house, next to my husband's OpenReach van. There's no livery on the side of my van — I was worried it might get broken into, if a potential thief knew about my tools inside it. And I also didn't want to attract too many new customers by putting contact details on the side. I can get easily swamped with phone calls if I advertise.

Inside the van are all the tools I've accumulated — pipe benders, soldering torches, drills, hand tools and more. There's way too much stuff in the van. Rob sometimes peers in, and marvels at the chaos. But despite appearances, everything has a home, and I can find what I need for my jobs.

In the bedroom upstairs, I can hear my children playing. I have two daughters, aged 11 and 12. When the time comes, when the Covid lockdown is over, I'll have a job — my own business — to go back to. There'll be a huge backlog of work. I'll be able to earn money again. I'm one of the lucky ones.

The rewards of being a self-employed plumber are numerous. I have the potential to earn good money. The work is interesting. I'm never bored. I'm always learning new things. I like my customers. I'm my own boss, and I've got freedom.

But there is a dark side to my job. Most things have a dark side. In my case, I worry a lot. I worry that I'll be out of my depth, which is a fair concern due to the complexity of my work.

Plumbing is not an easy job. There are usually problems to be overcome, and unexpected scenarios. I spend a lot of time planning jobs, downloading manuals, watching Youtube videos — everything I can do so that I go to my jobs prepared and informed. And that's a really good thing to do. But I lose perspective. I get in what I can best describe as a 'tizzy', and forget that I've been self-employed for several years, and have somehow muddled through a lot of difficult moments.

Monday mornings are always hard. I wake up feeling

sick, and anxious. My mind spins, asking 'what if?' What if I face a problem I can't cope with? I'll be on my own. What will I do? I lose all perspective — even if it's a simple tap replacement, I still fret. By the afternoon, I've generally calmed down. I'll then be OK for the rest of the week. Only for the cycle to return the following Monday.

Like most people, I've never liked uncertainty. But I force myself out. And I'm glad I do. Because the fear of what I might face is never as bad as what is actually out there. I can now do things I never imagined. I've been pushed to the limits of what I thought I could achieve, only to reach one peak and then progress to a higher one behind.

And I've had such an awesome adventure in the process. I've met so many inspiring people. I've learned so much — not just about plumbing, but about people, and about myself.

But I'm puzzled. Who am I? How did I get here? What kind of person — or kind of woman — does what I do?

Chapter 1

Jobs for the girls

If the world fell apart, what jobs would be left? And in particular, what jobs could a wife and mother do?

It was April, 2011. I'd just moved to Weymouth — a pretty seaside town on the south coast of the UK — with my then husband, (let's call him Ken, as he'll get peeved if I use his real name here), and our two toddlers.

Ken had just taken a job as sub-editor on the local newspaper, The Dorset Echo. I was also a journalist, but I didn't have a job.

"You know there's no future in the media," he said for the umpteenth time.

The kids were in bed. We sat on our mattress, on the floor of our new bedroom in our rented three-bedroom house, pondering the way ahead.

That morning, I'd wandered down to the beach with the kids, lost in thought. What would be the next big thing in my life? There was always a next big thing. I knew it was coming. And again, I wondered how wise our decision had been to give up our high-flying jobs in Sydney — where we'd lived for eight years — to rejoin our families in the UK.

Back in Australia, wages were higher. Competition for jobs was slightly easier. And I had landed my dream job with the Australian Daily Telegraph as an arts writer, covering top theatres and galleries and interviewing famous actors. But in Weymouth, there were no such jobs.

However, I knew something was out there for me, waiting to be discovered.

"Let's look at this again," said Ken. "The economy comes crashing down. And don't suggest website design again. What can't be outsourced to India, and what can't most people do themselves? What is always in demand, and is well-paid?"

"Oh, I don't know," I said, starting to get bored. "Plumbers? I guess I'll just have to be a plumber."

It was a throw-away comment. But as quickly as the words came out of my mouth, the idea jumped into my head. A plumber? Why not? Could women be plumbers? Could a 38-year-old female journalist make the switch?

I thought back to a poster on the wall of my youth club when I was a kid. It showed a group of women in jeans, checked shirts and hard-hats on a building site. Some carried tools. One leaned on the wall she was building. They were strong and confident. They looked like women who would play guitars around a campfire, chewing gum and drinking beer. They looked like a gang I might have liked to have joined, if I hadn't been scared of them.

But that was never going to happen. I was never going to meet these women. I didn't believe the poster's claims that girls could do anything. I didn't see any women on the building sites that sprung up near my childhood home in Essex. I didn't have any friends who wanted to be builders.

And besides, my parents told me girls weren't physically strong enough to do such jobs.

And that disappointed me. I loved the smell of workshops, and the smell of metal. I loved to know how things work.

If plumbing had been on my radar when I was 16, I might have trained for it back then. As it was, I was already interested in working with tools. My favourite subject at school was craft and design.

The careers teacher at school told us about apprenticeships. A prominent local employer made industrial air-conditioning units. They took on handfuls of youngsters each year and put them through a welding, engineering and machine maintenance training program. It looked like great fun, and led to a job at the end of it.

This same teacher — he also taught history — told my class that women shouldn't have careers. We should be at home, in the kitchen. Was he joking? I thought not. He said this in a serious voice. Nobody laughed. Nobody even blinked, so I'm not even sure anyone else heard him. My classmates might have zoned out. But I heard what he said. On top of this, the school map still labelled the various parts of the school as 'girls' craft' and 'boys' craft'.

Needless to say, I didn't feel particularly optimistic about such a tools-based apprenticeship. So I didn't investigate further, let alone apply. Which was probably for the best, looking back. I ended up with high grades in my GCSEs. I could go to sixth form college and study A levels, which is what I did. I chose A levels in maths, physics and CDT (craft/design/technology). Not many girls were studying these subjects — in both my design and physics classes, there were two girls (out of about 15 students). However, the tutors and students were very supportive of me and the other girls. It was quite refreshing after the old-fashioned attitudes at school.

My favourite subject was CDT. It involved building mock-ups of our designs. In the first term, we built battery-holders for our Walkmen (the days before iPods, when a Walkman was the size of a shoe box and would need six batteries to power it). Later in the course, I designed and built a pop-up darkroom in which to process black and white photographs.

"Hasn't your dad taught you to paint properly?" my tutors asked me one lunchtime. I was putting the final touches to my darkroom — it was to be painted black inside (to absorb stray light better).

"No," I replied.

I came from a traditional household. When my siblings

and I were small, in the 1970s, our mother stayed home to look after us while our father went off to work as a purchasing manager, then working for an international medical equipment company. Later, when I was about ten (and my brother eight, and sister six), our mother returned to work as a secretary.

Although our parents both worked full-time, our mother would cook the meals and stay up late doing housework while our father watched TV. But at the weekends, my father would fix the car or do the gardening while she enjoyed her free time. Or so the theory went. But my mother always seemed tired and irritable. She was always in a hurry. Always trying to make time for herself. If women worked so hard, I wasn't sure I wanted to grow up.

She was also frustrated that she didn't know how to fix things. Even silly things, like changing a light bulb, were a mystery to her. Once, she thought the TV was broken when it was on standby. My mother isn't a very technical person. So my father took care of that side of things. And he also tried to teach my brother DIY skills. On many a Sunday afternoon, my brother would be dragged out of his room, to help mow the lawn, trim the hedge, or fix the car. Every step of the way, he'd be moaning. He wanted to stay in his room, watching TV.

"Why don't the girls have to help?" he'd ask.

"Because they're girls," our father would reply. "They help your mother out."

Only we didn't. Aside from maybe tidying up after making a sandwich, neither of us did any cleaning or other chores. But when my mother went away for a weekend, to visit my aunt in Yorkshire, my father expected me to take over the household chores. It didn't go well. First, some washing needed putting on. My father must have loaded the machine, and didn't know how to turn it on. Neither did I. We both stood there, staring at it.

"What do you mean you don't know how to use it," he asked. "You're a girl of 15. That's ridiculous. Hasn't your mother shown you?"

No, she hadn't. And besides, I thought — not brave enough to say it out loud: "You're a man of 40 plus. You're three times my age."

The next day, our father decided we'd go ahead with the regular Sunday roast. Step 1: Get the ingredients together. I was summoned from my room, away from my homework, and sent to the local shop where I bought the required potatoes. We already had the meat.

But my task didn't end there. I was also expected to cook the dinner. A hunk of beef was already waiting for me in the fridge, along with some vegetables. Again, my father and I stared at the chunk of meat.

"It's your job to cook it," he said. "You're a girl. You should know how to do it."

"I've never cooked a roast dinner in my life," I said.

"Well, go next door and ask the neighbour how to do it," he replied.

I asked the neighbour — who had become a good friend of the family. She said to wrap it in tin foil and put it in the oven for a couple of hours. So that's what I did. I wrapped it up, bunged it in, and returned three or four hours later to retrieve it. It looked and smelled OK, so I was happy. I don't remember much about the vegetables, but I do know we all sat down to eat the meal.

Looking back, I dread to think what I served up. Because my father never again asked me to cook roast dinner. Even now, I struggle with a roast. It's as if part of my brain is missing. But these are the skills I have — or haven't — developed. And these skills go back to my school days, when I started to mould the future 'me' and my interests.

At age 18, towards the end of my A-level design course, I was fascinated with the college workshop. I spent most of my lunchtimes in it, either working on my projects or making random items.

My tutors taught me how to paint. They also taught me how to use various tools and machines in the workshop, including the welding equipment. And after that, I spent countless lunchtimes wrapped up in safety clothes, torch in hand. I don't remember what I made. I just liked welding bits of metal together.

Meanwhile, in my physics lessons, I learned how airplanes stayed in the air, how radiation and radio waves worked, and the calculations to fire a rocket into orbit. I was fascinated. In maths, I learned how to calculate the trajectories that kept missiles in the sky, and the speed that motorbikes had to go around a banked speed track. It was all fascinating stuff.

Ever the diligent student, I brought my work home with me. My bedroom became my workshop, which upset my father. He said that bedrooms were for sleeping in, and that I should do such work in the garage. But I preferred working in my bedroom, and admiring the growing constructions on my floor.

One project became so big that I trapped myself in my room for an evening — having built it butt up against the door.

My tutors had high hopes for me. A career in engineering was mentioned. But I was seriously tempted by architecture, which was also highly approved.

The careers suggested to me were always intellectual. Never hands-on. I was 'university material' and destined for a clever job in an office. And I suppose this would have been the same if I was a boy. The trades were never mentioned. They were seen as being for the kids that didn't make it to university.

But this was blinkered thinking on behalf of my teachers. The trades offer interesting, and well-paid careers. Some of the jobs are highly skilled, and need excellent technical knowledge, not to mention problem-solving and creativity. And the wages are higher — well, much higher than traditional women's work, such as nursing and childcare.

This is often the same for men. Some of my male

plumbing friends say that their former school friends who entered the trades are generally more affluent than those who went to college. Among my female school-friends, those without qualifications became carers, shop assistants, or worked in cafes. Others, with A levels, found jobs in offices. One of my best friends ended up in insurance, in London. At 19, she was buying smart suits and catching the train to the city every morning. She still seems so grown up and sophisticated compared to me.

Not so long ago, young women struggled to even access further education. My mother is a good example of wasted female talent. A bright and motivated girl, she got good grades in her 'O' levels and wanted to continue her studies, but didn't know what she wanted to do with her life. As it was, career options were limited.

"If I'd wanted to be a nurse or teacher, my parents might have let me go to college," she once told me. But she didn't want to be either of those things. Her parents felt higher education would be a waste of time.

"You'll only get married, and it will all have been for nothing" they told her. She was to leave school, and find a job. But my mum was resourceful. She bought a typewriter, and taught herself to type. Then she packed her bags, and got on the train to London. It was the swinging 60s. In London, she found work in a typing pool. She also found lots of parties — she met my father at a party.

My father had a better educational start in life. After passing the 11plus and going to grammar school, he went to technical college to study electronics and business studies. Then he embarked on a career as a purchasing manager.

It was always one of my mother's regrets that she hadn't had the opportunity for education. Such was the times. My birth certificate doesn't include a section for the mother's profession. In the past, just the father's job was asked for.

I'd certainly had many more career options open to

me than my mother, though not necessarily on the tools. If I were to learn a technical skill, it was made clear that I would be using it from my desk. But that was in the 1980s. What about today? Might the trades be more accessible to my daughters when they leave school? What are young women doing when they leave school these days?

According to UK government statistics, girls are getting higher grades in both GCSEs and A levels than their male counterparts. They are also more likely to stay in education after age 16.*2

And at UK universities, in 2021, more women than men enrolled in university. Though on some courses, men still outnumbered women. While more women than men studied veterinary science, psychology and medicine, higher proportions of men enrolled in engineering, technology and computer science.*3

Meanwhile, the plumbing industry is facing a skills shortage. More than 35 percent of gas engineers are aged from 56 to 65. As these people retire, not enough young people are taking their places. The trades seem to have forgotten about women.*4

In apprenticeships, more young women are going into construction. A study in 2021 found ten percent of construction apprentices to be female. This was a two percent increase from the previous year. *5

Other studies have found that increasing numbers of women have considered careers in the trades. In 2021, one study found that 21 percent of women in the UK had considered joining the trades in the previous 12 months. So the interest from women is there. Women want to be involved in building the world around them.

These women could be such an asset to the construction industry. Why are company bosses still overlooking such untapped potential? Why don't we see more women on building sites? Why aren't schools doing more to promote the trades to girls? It doesn't make sense.

From time to time, schemes to boost female entrants

pop up. Such as a Bristol-based housing association that launched a 'women in trades' initiative to help boost its numbers of female apprentices. In 2014, WaterSafe offered scholarships to help fund training for female plumbers.

Bit by bit, the industry is changing. Colleges are more accustomed to having female students onsite. During one course I attended, run by a boiler manufacturer, a fellow student told me that years ago, he never saw any female students. But now, at least one woman was often on the courses he attended.

On social media, it's more common to see plumbing posts by other women. And the language on the forums has changed to become more inclusive. More posts now begin with 'Lads and lasses...'

Social media has also brought women plumbers together, through Facebook women's plumbing groups. The mutual support is invaluable to women working in a male-dominated industry. Just knowing there are other women out there doing the same work as you is a boost. I feel less of an oddity. I feel more confident knowing that my gender doesn't stop me from doing the job I love.

But to the outside world, a female plumber is unusual. So few of us are out there, especially working at a high enough level where we could be role models to inspire the next generation. With so few female mentors in construction, how is a young girl to be inspired? How could she even imagine that she could find a brilliant career in the industry?

Not long ago, I got to hear about the mother of a 10-year-old girl. Her daughter had been laughed at by her classmates for declaring her ambition to be a plumber when she grew up. The child felt humiliated. Despite pointing out what an excellent career plumbing could be for her, she was mocked. Not even the teacher stood up for her. So I and other female plumbers jumped on our keyboards, and each wrote a message to her offering encouragement and support, proving that — as women ourselves – this was a great career for a girl to aspire to.

And at a grassroots level, people are trying to inspire young girls. Such as my local Girl Guides leader, who summons a group of tradeswomen every couple of years to spend an evening with her pack.

I asked my daughter for her thoughts on a technical career. She planned to take extra science options for her GCSEs, and wanted to be a scientist. Maybe even an astronaut. But definitely something to do with science.

"Aha," I said. "I suspect a fuse has gone in my car. The radio won't come on. Come and check it out with me. I'll show you how to use a multimeter."

But no. "Mummy, that's boring. I mean proper science. Not fixing cars or plumbing."

Plumbing just wasn't interesting. But at least she knew what a plumber was, which was more than I knew at her age. For despite learning so many technical things at school, I never learned about the world directly around me.

Not once did I question how water was supplied around the house. The boiler was invisible to me. I didn't know about the wall thermostat, or the gas meter with the emergency shut-off lever. None of this ever crossed my mind. Why isn't this taught in schools, as a core subject to all students?

Not much seems to have changed since I was a child. For while women have carved fantastic careers in the plumbing industry, we are still few and far between. I imagine that one day, she'll see a similar poster in her youth club, showing a bunch of women building a house. I spent four years looking at my poster.

I eventually concluded it could only come from some well-meaning but misguided bunch of feminists, whose ideals didn't match the real world. I wasn't going to be their guinea pig, putting my future career on the line as part of their political experiment.

I needed to see these women in the real-world. But on the building sites in my town, there were no women.

My science and workshop tutors at college were all male. I was praised for pushing the boundaries of what a girl could do, but I felt that I didn't fit in.

So after finishing my A levels, I abandoned the workshop and tools in favour of a career in the media. I went to university, and studied photography, and then journalism. I then spent the next few years sat in an office, working for a series of newspapers and magazines. I'd had an amazing time — eventually working on the arts pages of a mainstream Australian newspaper, and making regular trips to the Sydney Opera House for interviews.

But here I was, back in the UK, hundreds of theatre reviews and two children later, and ruminating over Armageddon. And what did I just say? How would we survive the end of the world? Did I say I'd have to be a plumber?

Whatever I'd said, the conversation had moved on. Ken was now talking about accumulating emergency food stocks, in case of a nuclear power plant exploding, or whatever, that might disrupt the supermarket supplies. But I hadn't forgotten what I'd said.

The next day, in between picking up Lego and changing nappies, I did a Google search on 'female plumbers.' A website run by an organisation called Stopcocks popped up. Based in Yorkshire, this was a fledgling organisation dedicated to helping women into the plumbing industry. For a monthly fee, members would receive technical support, educational and social events, and also business support.

Wow. So there were women out there doing this job. Maybe I wasn't delusional after all. So I dug around a bit more. I found the website of a woman in Essex, called Lisa, who was a self-employed plumber. She'd retrained at around the same age as me, following a technical career with a company that laid pipes and supply lines around the world.

Her contact details were on the website. Being a bit shy to pick up the phone, I emailed her, and explained I was considering re-training as a plumber. Could I phone her for advice? And then I went back to my Google search.

As I scrolled down, more websites and more articles about female plumbers followed. One of them was about a survey that had been done, showing that — given the choice — a significant number of older and female householders would prefer a female tradesperson. The main reasons were that they'd feel more comfortable inviting another woman into their homes. And they felt we'd be more trustworthy, and would tidy up after ourselves.

So, going back to the Armageddon check list: this job was in demand (with particular demand for women). It couldn't be outsourced overseas. Most people couldn't fix their own plumbing. I could be self-employed, and fit it around my family. And — better still — I could return to my first love of working with tools. How fantastic. I'd found my next big thing. So, how to proceed?

Chapter 2

The man who promised it all

So just how does one become a plumber? I didn't know. I grabbed my laptop, and logged onto Google. A load of fast-track plumbing courses aimed at adult learners popped up. I already knew about these colleges. Lisa — the woman from Essex, who I had emailed — had studied at one.

She'd been a star pupil at her college. Following an intensive few months of home-learning modules, and several weeks of classroom/workshop time at the college, she'd passed the basic plumbing theory exams.

To get the full qualifications, she'd need to compile an onsite portfolio of jobs, and have an assessor watch her at work. According to her website blurb, her logbook was still in progress. The important thing was that she was out there, plumbing. She'd shown it could be done, that a woman could re-train mid-career and enter the trades.

I got my pen and paper out. I needed to write a to-do list, starting with the required qualifications. I found them on a careers website.

NVQ2 Plumbing & Heating: This is the basic qualification for domestic plumbing. It covers bathroom installation, radiators and heating systems, waste pipes, guttering, and basic repairs.

NVQ3 Plumbing & Heating: The advanced plumbing qualification, which includes more commercial plumbing, system design, and advanced repairs and fault finding. It also has options such as gas, and renewables.

An email had come back from Lisa, inviting me to give her a ring — so I did. She told me more about her training.

"I'm a bit of a book worm," she said, mentioning that she'd read every page of every plumbing book that had come her way.

She'd also spent hours scouring the advice posts on numerous online plumbing forums. Admittedly, the leap from the classroom to the real world hadn't been easy for her. Lisa had started by renovating a friend's bathroom, for a minimal labour charge.

"It took about four weeks, which is a really long time," she said. "I was ridiculously slow. But I needed to give myself time to learn. I didn't want to just rush through, and risk not doing a good job."

At the sidelines was a family friend — a retired plumber — who would give her a hand if she hit any problems. And from there, she'd kept going. From taps and toilets, to blocked pipes and leaks, and then full bathroom refurbs, she'd take it on. And she was good at her job.

"I'm booked up four weeks in advance," she said, "Despite no advertising." Her entire customer base was word-of-mouth.

"I get better customers that way, who won't mess me around or not pay me."

She could pay the mortgage on her three-bedroom cottage, and had also recently treated herself to a large flat-screen television (after having reached a personal goal on her income).

"I'd love to come out plumbing with you one afternoon," I said, shyly. To which she replied "Of course. Any time."

The next day, I went back online and looked up the phone number of the training college she'd attended.

"How much money do you have?" asked the lady who answered the switchboard, getting straight down to the nitty-gritty. "Course fees are £7,000 for the full course."

I gulped. I knew it would be pricey. And this would eat up our savings. "Yes, I've got the money," I confirmed. Well, sort out … I'd sort that bit out later.

"Great," she said. "Shall I book you in for a consultation with our training advisor? We have one in your area, who can come to your home, and talk you through the course."

"OK."

And so it was, a week later, that a lanky, middle-aged man in a battered sports car and cowboy boots knocked on our door. And we got down to business.

Just to confirm, was it myself who wanted to do the plumbing training, he asked.

"Yes," I replied, feeling very bashful. It felt odd to say out loud. Surely it should have been my husband, a man, taking the hot seat for the training talk. But our visitor didn't consider it odd.

"We've had quite a few women come through our college," he said. "They've all been extremely competent plumbers, and have done extremely well."

And then he launched into a description of the course, and the various home-study and workshop modules.

I'd phoned my dad the day before, telling him of my investigations. My dad was sceptical.

"I'd think very carefully about such a move," he said. He didn't want to discuss his reasons.

"I need a new job," I said. "Any ideas what else might suit me."

Again, not much. "It's not easy to switch any career later on," he said.

If journalism wasn't coming up with the goods, maybe I could go shelf-stacking in the supermarket?

I was shocked. Was that all he thought I was good for? I was only 38. I had so much to offer, and so much potential to achieve whatever I wanted. Another family member was also sceptical.

"No one will give you a job," she stated. "And even if they do, you'll only end up unblocking toilets."

From my brother… no comment. He wasn't interested. But my mother was instantly behind me.

"Oh wow, I never know what you're going to do next," she exclaimed. "You'll be brilliant at whatever you put your mind to."

And Ken… a big yes. The idea of my returning to work, and potentially earning a shed load of money was a winner. He didn't care if I was plumbing, or indeed shelf stacking. It was the money that spoke.

And according to the training adviser in front of us, there were big bucks to make from plumbing.

"You can earn £70K a year as a plumber," he said.

I must have looked surprised.

"Really?"

"Yes, of course."

Ken had pound signs before his eyes. I recognised the look on his face — glassy eyes, and a blank expression.

"What, even in Weymouth?" I asked.

"Yes."

But this just wasn't true. Having done some prior research, I had good reason to doubt him. At the time, the UK average salary for an experienced plumber was £31,000. For gas engineers it was £37,500.

In London, some plumbers employed by big firms were on higher wages. But invariably they had to pay for their company vans, an apprentice and other overheads. It didn't reflect their take-home pay.

Having asked around, I knew the general salary (for an employed gas engineer) with a few years of experience in Weymouth was around £25,000. So the charlatan in front of us was selling us a fib.

He must have sensed from my non-committal 'mmmms' that I wasn't yet sold on the financial rewards. But then his trump card walked into the room. In came my youngest daughter, still aged only 18 months. Her father tried to pick her up, so I could better continue with my plumbing discussion. But the little girl wanted me, and insisted on running into my arms. Ever the salesman, our guest was quick to react.

"And you can study, and then work part-time," he said. "You can work the hours that suit you. You can be a mum, and you can be a plumber. You can be both."

I could choose the weeks that suited me for my college sessions. I'd do six blocks at the college, each a week long. And then I could do the home studies at my own pace, in the evenings, when the kids were in bed. Now that did sound good. But I kept my non-committal expression.

"Would the course be adequate?" I asked. "Would I be good enough to just go out plumbing, on my own?"

The course advisor (aka sales rep) looked affronted. But of course. What a stupid question, said his face. How could you possibly think otherwise?

"We'll get you up to the required standard," he said. "That's what we're here for. You'll be a fully qualified, competent plumber. And you'll have onsite experience — we have numerous partnerships with plumbing businesses that provide work experience to our students."

This time next year, I could be out there — depending on how quickly I wanted to work through the course.

But it was the work experience I wanted to know more about. Lisa had said to get as much hands-on experience as I could. Whenever. Whatever. I was to take every opportunity.

This work experience was the clincher, arguably just as valuable (if not more so) than time spent in the college workshops. Who were these partnered plumbing businesses? When and where could I get this experience? What would I be doing? Could I put my name down now, and get it planned in advance?

Our advisor was reluctant to give details. He didn't have them on him. But he could dig them out for me when he was back in the office. And with that, our meeting was concluded. We saw him to the door, and watched him drive away.

"I didn't like him," said Ken. Which surprised me, as he'd been seeming to lap up his every word.

"And the college is run by an investment bank." he continued. "He told me, as he was leaving. The college is all about profit."

Of course. Most things are about making money, I thought.

At playgroup that week, I thought more about the college. I wasn't convinced that a fast-track course was my best option. Time wasn't something I had a lot of. Not with two young children to look after. My life was a merry-go-round of playgroups, swim lessons, beach trips, bath-times, story sessions, and endlessly cleaning the floors and dinner table.

I was so busy with family life that I hadn't even picked up my guitar since our eldest daughter was born three years earlier. I'd used to play it every day. Likewise, my bike was covered in rust. How my life had changed.

My husband was also extremely busy. He was still working full-time at the local newspaper as a sub-editor (a job he hated, but it paid the bills.) And we had no family living nearby or friends or support networks. So the chances of me finding time for a fast-track course were remote. Nevertheless, I did some more research. I was enjoying looking into it all. But what I found wasn't encouraging.

Lots of former students were grumbling about fast-track plumbing courses. It seemed the grand promises of high incomes and great plumbing careers rarely eventuated. Lisa was an exception.

Many posts on the forums were from people who had taken out bank loans to pay for the course. Some had been left in crippling debt. One former student had re-mortgaged his house, and another had borrowed money from his family. Many weren't earning enough from their new careers to pay the debts, let alone support themselves.

I decided a fast-track course wasn't for me. I'd still be at home part-time with young children for the next two years, until they started school, so I had nothing to gain with a quick qualification. And I didn't want to cram so much information into my head so fast. Things stick better with me if learned over a longer period of time. So I approached my local colleges.

By luck, I was in time to enrol with the next intake of students on the introductory plumbing course at Kingston Maurward College, in Dorchester, which would start that September. I'd be studying alongside school leavers and apprentices, one day a week. And as a bonus, the course fees would be about half of that of the fast-track colleges.

My plan of action fell into place. I would enrol in a plumbing course at my local college, and I would organise my own work experience. I would make friends with local plumbers, and ask them to take me out with them. That is how I would do it. If only it would be that easy.

If I'd known how bumpy the road ahead would be, and how much hard work, luck and courage would be needed, I could never have started on such a radical career change.

Chapter 3

Just a girl

There's a song by the pop star Gwen Stefani, that goes: "Cos I'm just a girl, Oh little old me, Well don't let me out of your sight. Oh I'm just a girl, all pretty and petite, so don't let me have any rights."

It's a powerful song about a young girl trapped by stereotypes of femininity, and wanting her freedom. It came onto our radios in 1995. It became a hit, and helped Gwen's band — No Doubt — break into the mainstream.

It was certainly a song that resonated with me. So many times, I'd been told that I was 'just a girl', especially when I was growing up in the 1980s. I don't hear the phrase much these days — we've become more politically correct. But the lower expectations for women remain in other expressions such as: "You run/throw/cry like a little girl."

The other thing I often heard when I was a child was: "Are you a boy or a girl?" When I was ten years old, this was a familiar question. My hair was short, and I wore jeans and a jumper. My gender wasn't obvious.

On one occasion, I was in a pub beer garden with my family. The adults sat indoors, while the children congregated around the swings and see-saw. The question popped up again. I sensed that the boy in front of me wouldn't want to play with me if I told him the truth. So I lied.

"I'm a boy."

There. I said my name was John. He looked happy.

Now that was out of the way, we could hang out for a bit, before our parents decided it was time to go.

My days of lying were numbered. I knew that puberty would soon be upon me, and I wouldn't be able to hide my gender for much longer. But I was furious that my gender should be such an issue.

Behind my tomboy clothes and banter, I felt unseen. The adult world was telling me that being a girl was bad. So did that make me bad? How could I be written off so easily? I had school friends that were girls and boys. They were all so different and unique. How could someone be so quickly categorised and discarded, based on their gender? I didn't get it.

On that occasion, in the beer garden, I got away with my ruse. My younger brother and sister were elsewhere in the playground, so they didn't blow my cover.

"You're just a girl."

My father would declare it, supposedly in jest. He'd come out with random statements as we passed by in the house. When I'd protest, he'd say he was joking. That I shouldn't take it seriously. But this was serious. I'd heard about female babies being left to die in the fields in India. This was very serious.

Other times, he'd be surprised to see women bus drivers. There must have been some recruitment drive in our town that targeted women, as all of a sudden it seemed that women bus drivers were everywhere. I didn't see what the big deal was.

My hobbies as a child were wide-ranging. I loved reading books. I loved art and craft. And knitting. All 'normal' activities for a girl. But I also liked to build dens in the forest near where I lived. I'd go swimming in the local river. I had a train set and would spend hours sculpting papier-mache hills around it. I was fascinated with computers, and read books about computer programming. Such as my enthusiasm, I even won a trip to visit a mainframe computer, IBM in Hitchin, which was one of the best days of my childhood.

I also liked to play football. But when the boys at school complained, the headmaster told me and my best friend we shouldn't be on the field. That football was for the boys.

At secondary school, we could study domestic science or metal/woodwork. If we were in any doubt, the map of the school given to us on our first day marked these classrooms as 'girls' craft' and 'boys' craft.'

Most girls chose the cookery and needlework option, saying it would be the most useful in their adult lives. But while these are essential skills, they are valuable to both men and women. Likewise with metal and woodwork. We all benefit from basic skills in these subjects. I chose metalwork, and I still have a sculptured bumblebee with a screw-thread tail that I made in that class.

Another memorable event from my childhood came during a joint Girl Guides/ Boy Scouts camp. The boys were going on an afternoon trip down some caves, with helmets and headlamps. This sounded like great fun. But it was just for the boys. The girls, meanwhile, stayed at the camp and prepared food. I spent the afternoon peeling potatoes and cleaning soot off the pans. I assumed the girls' caving trip would follow later in the week. But it didn't. Nor any other girls-only trip.

I was livid. I'd have loved to go caving. Why would they think that being a girl would mean that wouldn't appeal to me? It was just my thing. And I was so confused. Why were girls locked out of fun things? And why was being female so bad? Why was my gender so criticised? I wanted to be accepted, and to be liked. But I seemed to be beaten before I'd even begun.

When puberty inevitably arrived, I embraced femininity. Almost overnight, my world changed. I enjoyed dressing like a young girl and being different from the boys.

"Sit still," my friend Vicky would instruct me as she'd try out her mother's make-up on me. She'd gone from dressing up her dolls to dressing up me.

With other friends, I'd scour the pop magazines for the latest boy bands and explore the high-street fashion shops at weekends. Suddenly, I didn't want to hang out with boys anymore. Or at least not boys my age. They were alien and different. They were small, spotty and squeaked when they talked. They weren't fun anymore. But still I worried about growing up, and becoming a woman.

"What are those?" A family friend laughed at me one day, pointing at my chest.

Likewise, the boys at school had noticed them too. They'd try to ping the girls' bra straps to ascertain who was wearing a bra. From then on, I wore baggy jumpers — even in summer, even if I got hot. I especially wore a jumper if I was out jogging, as the wind would push the fabric tight to my skin and show my curves.

And so I progressed into my teenage years. I focussed on my studies. This was another source of frustration.

At 16, I was predicted lower than average grades in my GCSEs. This angered me. Why didn't my teachers think I was capable of more? Surely it was because they hadn't taken time to get to know me. I was just the quiet kid at the back of the class. Unseen. So I acquired the textbooks, and studied — hard. But my efforts seemed to go unnoticed.

In physics, the teachers said I wasn't capable of sitting the higher exam paper — which would have opened up potentially higher grades. This was because I'd flunked the mock exam — a single exam, taken a year previously, that I'd originally missed due to illness, and that I'd eventually taken surrounded by a classroom of rowdy teenagers who left me unable to concentrate.

This was an issue, as I wanted to continue my physics studies at A level. I knew I was as good as the boys in my class, who were taking the higher papers. So I asked to re-sit the mock exam, or sit any other test to prove my worth. If I failed any further tests, I'd submit quietly. But they wouldn't budge. I ended up sitting the lower paper, and — yet again — I was furious, when I finished the exam and left the hall.

"How did the exam go?" asked my physics teacher.

"It was easy. Ridiculously easy." I replied, seething.

And it had been. I knew I was capable of more, but hadn't been given the chance to show what I could do.

"The higher paper was tough," he said. "You'd have struggled with it."

And then something curious happened. In August, when my grades came through, the exam board had awarded me a B. My lower paper should have capped me at a C. I must have got 100 percent, or not far off, for such special dispensation.

At around that time, my school also arranged for me to go on a series of work experience placements, to help me decide what career might interest me. I liked art, so I was sent to the offices of a graphic designer. Unfortunately, the designer was off sick for the entire two weeks.

The women in the office decided I shouldn't waste my time drawing pictures and posters. I was shown a filing cabinet and told to sort the folders and documents, which is what I did. Would they have asked a young boy to do this? I'm not sure they would have. The work would have been seen as unworthy of a young man's potential and ambition, and a waste of his time. Whereas for me, the message I got was to face reality and not to think of myself as somehow better than the other females in the office. I didn't even get paid for my work.

A couple of weeks later, I visited the design offices of an industrial fan manufacturer. The man who showed me around generously thought women could do the job. But he didn't think we should get equal pay for it.

"Women's wages are just pin money," he said. "No way should they get the same money as men."

In the late 1980s, this was already an outdated attitude. The Equal Pay Act 1970 was supposed to prohibit less favourable employment conditions based on gender. But behind closed doors, this attitude persisted.

When I look back on all this, it's no surprise if women grow up feeling second-class and lacking in confidence. Girls from my generation were on a back foot before we even began, having to level up to debilitating stereotypes and low expectations of what we might achieve.

I grew up chasing perfection. I felt that if I wasn't good enough, the problem must lie with myself, and I had to try harder. It's a common sentiment among women that we must be twice as good as men to be valued equally. That is especially true when you venture onto traditional male territory. I grew up confused about gender stereotypes, and why it was such a big deal to be born either a man or a woman.

Luckily, though, the 1990s rolled along. It was the era of Britpop and an era of an influx of female-fronted indie bands — such as No Doubt, Sleeper, Texas, Garbage, The Cranberries, Skin, Hole, and many more. Big trainers and cargo pants were in fashion, which delighted me.

I spent a year at my local art school — where nobody cared what gender you were. The colour of your hair was of far more interest. And then I went to Derby university to study photography. My photography course had equal numbers of men and women. More applications were received from men. However the tutors wanted a gender balance. Other than lectures on gender studies in art, gender wasn't of much interest.

And this was so refreshing. I finally felt like I could be myself. I was young, and living away from home for the first time. The world was out there, for me to discover. It was such an adventure.

Each summer, I returned home to Essex, looking for a few weeks of paid work to bolster my student grant. For the first two summers, I picked apples. But I managed to get sacked, after handling the fruit too roughly and bruising it. In the third summer, I sold ice cream in a kiosk at the local zoo. But my favourite summer job came a few years later. By then, I'd finished my photography degree, and had taken a series of menial jobs to fund a backpacking trip first to Israel, and then to South America. I was due to return to university to study journalism, but I needed to earn some quick cash first.

The local job centre had a vacancy for a gardener. The advert said male or female (it was illegal to discriminate). I took the card to the job-centre advisor and asked if I could apply. He laughed. I said I was serious, so he shrugged his shoulders and gave me the details. I'd never gardened in my life (except for mowing my parents' lawn and growing a few sunflowers.) But experience wasn't necessary. It said so, in the advert. This was a basic job of mowing lawns and weeding, which I could handle. And it said male OR female. So I applied.

And so it was that the following week, I sat in the office of a property developer. He eyed me suspiciously. His last gardener had been sacked after falling asleep on the job. Was I up to the task? It was hard, physical work.

"Oh yes," I said, full of bravado.

It was raining outside, and oddly that always makes me feel energised and cocky. At that time, I was extremely fit and strong, and young — I was still only 25. I leaned back in my chair. "I can do it, no problem," I declared.

He seemed surprised, but also impressed. And I now know that that attitude would have appealed to him, and challenged him. He gave me a week's trial. I spent the entire week with a pair of secateurs, trimming a hedge on the grounds of a property he was having built.

The job was tedious. But it paid £6 per hour (far more than the other summer jobs on offer). Plus I was out in the fresh air, and could listen to my Walkman with no interruptions. So I was happy.

There must have been quicker ways to cut the hedge — an electric hedge cutter could have dealt with it in hours. But I'd been asked to cut it by hand, which is what I did.

My boss's new family home was going up at the other

end of the field. I could see the builders, and knew I was being watched. I daren't be seen slacking. Outside my lunch breaks, I didn't stop once, which was what was reported back to my new boss.

"Where did you find her?" the builders asked. "She doesn't stop."

And so I passed the trial, and was given more interesting work. I was sent to work at his current family home - a large property with a huge driveway, massive gardens, a tennis court, a veggie plot, a golf course, and a meadow for him to land his microlight aircraft in. I'd never seen such a big house and garden.

I would be working with three other gardeners — a middle-aged head gardener, a youngish bloke and an old part-time bloke. We even had our own tea hut. The blokes were lovely. I enjoyed working with them. But being the new kid, I had to prove my worth to them.

On my first day, I was asked to dig a flowerbed with the older man, who looked so old I was sure he must be in his early 80s. It was the beginning of summer, and the weather was quite warm. We both broke into a sweat as we dug the soil, neither stopping to rest, and both feeling the exertion. I felt the pressure to show I was physically up to the challenge. He also kept going strong. By the end of the day, we were both knackered. After that, we didn't compete again — neither of us could keep up such a pace.

I soon settled into my new job. My days would start with watering the plants in the back garden and patio, which took about an hour as there were a lot of them.

I then typically mowed one of the lawns, which was my favourite task. It always involved a ride-on mower. After being instructed not to turn it sharply on hills (in case it should topple over) and to be careful of ditches (a previous gardener had driven it into one), I was set loose. And I loved it.

I was also taught to drive the tractor, which had attachments on the back to mow the meadow.

Unfortunately, that field only needed cutting every few weeks. But it was great fun to do.

And I learned to rely on myself more. On my first day with the tractor, I had to get it through a gate. I'd only learned to drive a car a couple of years earlier, and wasn't great with squeezing any vehicle through a narrow space. But the tea-hut and my companions were a ten-minute walk away. And my pride also said I should drive it through myself.

Which is what I did. I lined it up with the gate. I knew it should get through, as the tractor had previously been in the field. It was tight, with only a couple of inches clearance of the rotor blades. But after checking my alignment, I drove it through with no issues.

Later, I drove the tractor back to the shed, and came across my boss. He had some visitors with him. He stopped me, and beckoned me down from the tractor as he proudly showed me to his companions. And I was proud too. Even if it was a little patronising, as he wouldn't have treated a male employee like that. I was marvelled over because I was female. I'd challenged the stereotypes of what a woman could do. And in the future, it would happen a lot more.

Chapter 4

Breaking stereotypes

How would I be different if I was a man? I'd probably be earning more money, for a start. In 2022, in the UK, government figures showed that women were paid just 90p for every £1 made by men. This was an average. Step into construction and this fell to just 76p for female employees. *7

Why? Might this be because few women are working on the tools? Maybe the women in construction are mainly doing low-paid admin work.

Or perhaps the industry is as archaic as the figures suggest, and women routinely are not receiving equal wages for equal work. But with so few women on the tools, it's difficult to get enough statistics for an accurate picture.

I dig a bit deeper. The gender pay gap starts early. According to a study by Starling Bank, girls get 20 percent less pocket money than boys, and pay 5 percent more for their toys. *8

Money is an indicator of how much value is given to a person. I'd always felt undervalued, and underpaid. Yes, blokes feel this too. But I'd always felt the weight of my gender. Like a heavy, sparkly pink shackle. GIRL. And all the stereotypes and expectations that go with that.

From the moment we are conceived, the world is obsessed with gender. What sex will the unborn baby be? Shall I buy it a pink or blue outfit? A doll or a toy car? Does it even matter? Are boys and girls really so different? Do we need to make such a big deal of gender? Human beings love to categorise. It makes our lives easier to manage. The world becomes a more dependable place when we know how people act. And we cling to those differences.

When scientists have found gender differences (other than our obvious, physical bodies), they are sometimes so slight that they are barely worth acknowledging. Our brains aren't so different — give neuroscientists a brain, and they can't tell if it is male or female.

Neuroscience is still in its infancy. There is so much to be discovered about how our brains and bodies work. To pull out snippets from studies, and extrapolate grand claims about gender differences is premature. And dangerous.

Yes, there might be biological differences that influence our behaviour. But how those differences are interpreted makes me uncomfortable. The claims made by so-called experts can have sweeping effects on our lives.I love science. I love maths. I love fixing things, and I love plumbing. And I'm female. Not so long ago, I would have been barred from such pursuits because of my gender. And what a shame that would have been.

Men and women are very different. Precisely what those differences are has been debated for centuries. To deny these differences exist is harmful to women. To do this may create a male 'default', putting women under pressure to be more man-like (whatever the current fashion considers that to be), and to withdraw any specific support that women need.

But on the other hand, stereotypes can take these differences too far. We can become lazy, and sometimes form tight ideas about men and women. Throw in age, class, culture, religion, and chosen profession — such as plumbing — and some of the stereotypes can become quite ridiculous.

One of my plumbing tutors was convinced that I must be a rugby player. It was around the time of the women's rugby World Cup, in 2014, and a lot of media attention was given to the UK team — which featured a female plumber. In my tutor's mind, all female plumbers played rugby.

"But I don't," I said. "I've never played rugby. Maybe tag rugby. But not proper rugby."

He didn't believe me. I didn't fit his stereotype. But finally, I convinced him. "Have you seen the size of some of those girls?" I asked. "I wouldn't last five minutes."

He looked me up and down. I was athletic, reasonably strong, and of fairly average height and build for a woman. But I wouldn't be the first choice for a rugby team.

"Fair enough," he said, finally convinced.

His was an isolated stereotype, formed by his own views of the world — or rather, from what he'd seen on the telly.

But whether we mean to or not, we teach our children to share our views — and stereotypes — of the genders. They grow up believing in those gender differences, eventually cemented through the school subjects and hobbies they follow. *9

Girls and boys have traditionally been socialised to develop specific skills. Science is full of contradicting studies regarding the possible differences between males' and females' innate abilities in mathematical, spacial, or language skills.

Though it seems near impossible to separate socialisation from the experiments. Studies on young children suggest that both genders brains work in similar ways, and that have the same potential to master a wide range of skills and interests. *10

So — as is the case in the UK — schools should teach and encourage a wide range of subjects to all pupils. So that we bring up well-rounded adults with a good spread of skills.

While some schools are still looking at gender-based learning styles, other schools — typically primary schools — have pushed to remove gender from the classroom.

But young children quickly learn which group (boys or girls) they belong to. They know which toys are for them, and which activities are for them. They're learning about the world, and looking for rules that will help them make sense of it all. The concern is that by dividing children by gender, they look for common traits to define their group, which can be limiting.

Experiments have found that by removing gendered language from classrooms, children are less likely to make sweeping generalisations about gender. After four weeks, one study found that boys and girls were less likely to say that only men could be doctors, or president of the United States. Their worlds opened up. *11

So 'boys to the left, girls to the right,' and so on, could be holding children back.

Moving away from these stereotypes opens up more diversity. Feeling like a misfit is no fun. We generally want to fit in with our peers. So pulling down the girl and boy stereotypes is a good place to begin.

An Australian PHD student, Dr Karen Struthers, looked into this further, as part of a thesis examining why there are so few women in construction. It makes interesting reading.*12

She went into schools, and asked the girls (aged 15 to 18) why they weren't enrolling in male-dominated courses — and especially trade courses such as metalwork and woodwork. A common response was that the girls felt uncomfortable being outnumbered in the classroom.

"If you are the only one, you feel intimidated," was one reply.

She then asked about their career choices, and whether they'd consider a career in the trades. The responses were positive. The girls weren't dismissing the trades as a career option. Rather, they either hadn't considered it or knew little about such careers.

One student said: "More girls would do it (male-dominated trades) if we knew more about it — if we had a lot more exposure to it to find out what it's really like."

The girls found the gender stereotypes really powerful. If a skill was perceived as only for boys, the girls were less likely to want to do it. There was also a perception that the trades were "not as good as uni." Trades were often seen as being for boys who didn't do well at school, and seen as an 'under-qualification.' The exception was parents who had trade experience, and recognised the value of such a career path.

Unsurprisingly, parents play a key role in their children's career choices. The parents that Dr Struthers spoke to recognised that girls can do all trades. And that's a good start. Maybe progress has been made after all.

When I was young, I found it difficult to get my parents' approval on my career choices. As my school years ended, I had to choose a career. I wanted to do something practical and fun.

A musician?

"No," said my mother. She asked how I would juggle being a mother and being on tour with an orchestra. And besides, my trumpet teacher said I wasn't good enough. And also that there weren't many professional female trumpet players out there. The idea was thrown out.

An electrician?

"No, you're a girl. You're not strong enough."

An architect? "Yes, you're a clever girl. You could do that."

My school arranged for me to spend an afternoon with a female architect (presumably to inspire me). She was designing the drainage for a house extension. I wanted to design big, public buildings. Her job looked dull and mundane. So I dropped the architecture idea.

My dad suggested pharmacology or business. I didn't know what either of those entailed. They didn't sound very interesting.

In the end, I settled on a one-year course in art and design. I then went to university to study photography, and then journalism. There were plenty of women in the media industry. I was confident I'd made a sensible choice.

But what about girls who want to go into construction — including plumbing? I was one of those girls. Although I loved my journalism career, I always felt I'd been shut off from other avenues at a young age. I'd taken A levels in maths, science and technology, yet the enticing trades door had seemed inaccessible.

Dr Struthers's study suggested that female role models and mentors would help encourage girls into the trades. I would have found that useful. But one-off examples aren't enough. It's not convincing. The exposure needs to be greater, and more sustained, to be meaningful.

Why is that, you ask? Because gender stereotypes are extremely difficult to change — even with young children. Researchers have played around with stereotypes in schools, with experiments that look at how entrenched stereotypes are in children. *12

One experiment involved reading a book to children, which swapped around stereotypes. The book featured a picture of a man in front of a stove, and said that he liked to cook dinner for his family. But the children later remembered the character as being a woman. Similarly, another story which featured a male cook in a hospital. The character was later remembered as being a doctor.

According to the research, dragging out one-off examples of male cooks — or female plumbers — doesn't work. Our minds are too good at filtering out the exceptions so that we can cling to our preconceived rules. We ignore what doesn't fit the mould.

Even within my own family, these gender rules are observed. I'm seen as an anomaly. My husband Rob always buys traditional boy toys for his toddler grandson. He insists he won't like dolls. And likely he won't, as he'll already know not to play with them. Rob also tells me that most women aren't interested in technical matters, overlooking the fact that I am a woman.

"You don't count," he says.

But I should count. I love technical things. I'm a woman. So surely this should put his assumptions in doubt.

By his thinking, toy guns would also be for boys. But it would appear girls are also keen to play at being soldiers. A third of the attendees at my youngest daughter's army cadet camp were female. They had great fun learning how to handle weapons, and run around in mock battle.

I've also bought tools for my daughters, who now own numerous hammers and toolboxes filled with screwdrivers and wrenches. But Rob sticks to his stereotypes, as do a lot of people.

"Girls don't like to get their hands dirty," he also says.

But we do. Or some of us do. Traditional female jobs such as childcare, nursing, cooking and cleaning all involve manual, hands-on tasks that can be dirty. Hobbies such as gardening, painting and pottery are also potentially grubby.

"It depends what you're putting your hands into," says my eldest daughter. "I don't like putting my hands in poo."

Neither do I. But otherwise, I don't mind getting dirty hands. I just wash them afterwards. But attitudes about suitable jobs for men and women are changing.

In my lifetime, women have increasingly found more opportunities in traditional male jobs. I see more women driving buses, flying planes, and joining the army than when I was young. And more men are entering the caring and nursing professions — I had two male midwives when I gave birth to my first daughter, in 2008.

More women — girls and adults — are considering careers in the trades, as a survey by accounts specialists Powered Now found.*6 Following the Covid pandemic, in 2021, on their website they wrote:

"While many people will be struggling to look for positives over the past year, it seems there is a big trend that needs shouting about. This International Women's Day [2021] we are delighted to reveal the findings from some recent research we have conducted.

"During the past 12 months 21% of women in the UK have considered a career in the trade. In a turn of events, the pandemic has highlighted that the trades is a haven for employment, and perhaps has been an unexpected catalyst to help move the industry closer to gender parity.

"While it isn't often that you associate International Women's Day with construction. Hopefully, people will start to recognise the careers in this industry are indeed available to women."

To encourage more women into the trades, more female role models and mentors are needed. The incomers need to know that they aren't one-offs, but part of a growing number of talented, and highly-trained and competent tradeswomen. And albeit slow, progress is being made.

In particular, more trades adverts on TV are featuring women.British Gas initially featured an advert which included a female engineer getting ready to go out to work in the morning. The advert caught my attention, as I wasn't used to seeing women gas engineers on TV.

Since then, diversity has grown, with other industry TV adverts — such as Check-A-Trade and Screwfix — also including female workers. It's a drip drip exposure, making us more accustomed to seeing tradeswomen. We'll soon expect to see women on those adverts. It will seem odd if they're not included.

Gender stereotypes continue to be questioned. But progress, since I was young, seems to have both gone forwards and backwards. The pressure on young people to comply with stereotypes seems so much more intense, largely due to the visual nature of the Internet and social media. Much of this concerns beauty ideals (women) and physical strength (men).

But on the other hand, men and women increasingly have greater options for alternative careers and lifestyles. There is more acceptance of young people who don't tick the heterosexual box. And more acceptance for choosing a non-traditional career.

My daughters tell me about several pupils at their school who identify as non-binary (neither boy or girl) or as transgender. It's a complex issue for a lot of young people, and is an issue I don't fully understand. But I appreciate why some of them are fed up with being identified by their gender, and the baggage that goes along with that.

When I was growing up, I didn't feel like I matched the 'woman' stereotype. And neither was I a man. I just wanted to be 'Jennie'.

What a shame that the stereotypes can still feel so claustrophobic. What a shame these young people don't feel they can be a 'man' or 'woman' and also have the freedom to discover, and be, themselves.

So how would I be different, if I was a man? Or — to be more accurate in modern times — if I'd been born into a biologically male body?

This isn't easy to answer. Life experiences may have altered me. Like the butterfly effect, change one thing in our histories — even a little thing — and huge changes can eventuate. Picking out where my gender and my uniqueness as a person begins and ends is near impossible.

This tangle is why we need greater freedom from gender stereotypes to discover ourselves, and find what —as individuals — we are capable of, and where our talents lie. And with such freedom, wondering how life would be different if I was a man starts to become less relevant.

Chapter 5

Back to college

Life used to be such a predictable roadmap from birth to death. I saw it as a fixed order, like a tick list: school, college, career job, marriage, children, more career and then retirement.

I thought I'd trundle through the list like a parcel on a conveyor belt. But as the years passed, I realised that life isn't so straightforward. A university degree isn't a magic key to a high-paying, fulfilling job. And that working hard for a company doesn't always bring rewards — sometimes just exploitation.

Gone are the jobs for life, and the employment security enjoyed by our parents. Gone are the days when a young woman (ie, my mother) could walk into an employment bureau and leave with a job. That's how she describes the '60s. It's brutal out there now.

Unsurprisingly, today's graduates are more likely to jump careers. One study found that more than half of Brits plan to change careers in the next five years. *13.

It makes sense to reinvent ourselves before we are pushed, to find ways ahead while we still have a chance to plan and invest in ourselves. So with this in mind, at 38, I returned to college to study plumbing. And I loved it.

Kingston Maurward College, just outside Dorchester, was where I went. It's mainly an agricultural college, where students learn to drive tractors, and care for horses and other animals. There is also a lake filled with budding outdoor pursuits instructors. At weekends, the gardens host weddings and other functions. It was a fun and beautiful place to be.

It was also the only college that would take me. At the time, in 2011, many colleges were only taking students through apprenticeship programs, who had workplaces where they could get hands-on experience for the logbooks. But this course was run by a former plumber, Dan Woods, who was keen to make the industry accessible to a wider range of people.

"Plumbing is a great career," he told me, during my initial interview. I'd been without childcare that day, and had taken my two young children with me. They sat sucking lollies as we talked. "There has to be a way in for people, if this is what they want to do," he said.

He had run a separate course the previous year for mature students (i.e., anyone over 25). But funding cuts had made it too expensive to run, so all students were now thrown in together. I'd be joined by a roofer (late 20s) and a retail worker (also in his 20s). The rest of the students would be 16-year-olds on formal apprenticeships. Sometimes, my classmates might have to brush up on key skills (i.e., English and maths), but otherwise we'd sit the same lessons, do the same tasks and sit the same exams.

It was a world away from my previous world of journalism and playgroups. But the excitement overcame my nerves as I dropped my children off at creche, and drove to college on my first morning.

Our plumbing workshop was at the back of the college grounds, surrounded by fields, allotments and a pond garden. I spent the first morning learning about the various pipe fittings. There were many names to remember: soldered tees, compression couplers, street elbows. Dan was intrigued to see me taking notes.

'I don't see many notepads in here,' he remarked. 'But it's a great idea. I wish more students would write things down.'

That afternoon, I had a go at soldering my first pipes. Looking back, it's incredible to think how nervous I was to light the soldering torch for the first time. I was seriously crapping myself, as the flame (only about an inch long) shot out of the nozzle.

Later that week, I bought myself a soldering torch and practiced soldering some joints in my backyard. And I started to feel more confident about using it.

Next came pipe bending. We made flat frames out of pipes, following instructions for offsets, cross-overs and connections. That, too, was fun.

I liked the lads on the course. They were young, and funny. They talked a lot about skateboarding, driving their cars, and computer games. But they also talked about dating and girlfriends, their parents, nights out on the town, money, jobs, etc.

College was often lively. Being student plumbers, sometimes the floor got wet. Dan kept a broom handy, to sweep the water out of the building. Once we were all so busy we didn't notice one of our colleagues squatting by a hot water cylinder, having just cut the wrong bit off the pipe and having plugged the open pipe end with his thumb. He was there for about half an hour.

During my two years at Kingston Maurward, I looked up more female plumbers. "Could I come out plumbing with you sometime?" I asked.

I needed to see other women plumbers at work, so I'd know it was a job that women could do. I also needed to see real-life plumbing, as there was a world of difference in making up a fitting at the comfort of a workbench, and then making the same fitting while squashed under a kitchen worktop.

The women I spoke to were friendly and supportive, and I spent many days out plumbing with them. One lived near my parents in Essex. Her work mainly consisted of bathroom installs and tap/toilet repairs. Come school and college holidays, I'd leave my children with my parents while I went out plumbing with her for the day. I'd sit behind her with my camera and notepad, documenting her every move. I learned loads.

Another female duo worked in Bournemouth. Similarly, I spent a few afternoons shadowing them. I was pretty useless. I spent half an hour trying to drill a hole in the floorboards. The battery was nearly dead in the drill, which was why it was spinning so slowly. It was my first time using a battery drill, so I wouldn't have known. They also showed me how to hang my first radiator, and I also smashed my first tiles off a bathroom wall.

But I needed more work experience, and closer to home. It was too time-consuming and expensive to travel up to two hours in rush hour traffic in the morning to Bournemouth.

Feeling reassured that women could be plumbers, and that I hadn't been a total idiot in my ambitions, I looked for local male plumbers to go out with.

Often, student plumbers struggle to find work experience placements. And it isn't easy. Most people I asked either said no or didn't reply. After all, what's in it for the plumber? They have a curious student in tow who will slow them down with questions, and be slow and inept at any practical task given to them.

So I tried to make it personal. I approached people whom I'd already got a connection with (such as having phoned for career advice), or whom were friends of friends (ie, you're friends with my mate, can I come plumbing? They'd look mean to say no). I also approached neighbours who were plumbers.

Most still said no or ignored me, but a couple were up for it. But only now and again. So I looked to make numerous plumbing friends, who I'd spread my time between.

The months passed, and my experience and skills grew. I got through my first year at college, and signed up for year two. That meant another round of course fees to pay.

I was skint. Ken and I had been surviving on one wage

for the past two years. Despite meticulous budgeting, we were going backwards each month. And I was so careful with money.

I'd buy the children's clothes from a charity shop. We skipped ice cream on days out and had homemade lollies from our freezer. I even bartered an hour's photo shoot for a magic show at my daughter's backyard birthday party. Holidays were taken on budget campsites. But we still couldn't make ends meet.

And I had no overdraft option on my bank account. My bank had slashed my overdraft facilities because I had no wages coming in. What remained would be charged at £1 per day, plus interest. I wouldn't have been able to pay an overdraft off. I daren't put my family's financial security in jeopardy. So I looked for alternative funding.

I found a charity called the Hilda Martindale Trust. Born in 1875, Hilda was one of the UK's first female civil servants. She studied hygiene and sanitation, and worked as a factory inspector for more than 30 years. She was particularly concerned with the working conditions of women. When she died in 1952, she left a trust fund to make awards to women who wanted to pursue a career that would be of value to their community. I ticked all the boxes, so I applied.

I cried when I received a text message telling me I'd been accepted for a grant. I was so relieved. I'd be given £1500 in instalments. So back I went to college. Year two started, and I began to compile the all-important college logbook. I asked my mentors to sign forms and photos confirming my onsite work with them.

The logbook requirements were very specific. Earlier assignments asked me to change a stop tap, install a bath, hang a radiator and pipe it up, etc. Later on, the tasks would be more difficult.

Towards the end of my second year, I came across a woman online who was looking for second-hand radiators. She was doing her house up on a budget.

She'd need someone to install them. I told her about my studies and my logbook, and offered my services for free (although she'd have to pay for the materials). Predictably, she jumped at the opportunity for free plumbing.

And so I installed my first radiator, on my own, in somebody's house. By then, I'd hung several at college, and some with other plumbers. I was confident I could do it. And so off I went to do it. I drained down the heating system, installed two new radiators, filled up the system and checked for leaks. All good. And I signed off a massive chunk of my logbook.

Back at college, I was also doing well. I was at the top of my class in the exams. Female plumbing students tend to study hard, and do well academically. And that was the case with me. When the exam results were announced, I'd shrug and pretend I wasn't that fussed. It wouldn't have gone down well for me to boast. But inside, I was singing and dancing. I'm naturally competitive, even if I don't always show it.

But while the boys on my course didn't open their books much, they were out plumbing daily. Their skills and abilities varied, depending on the opportunities given to them by their employers. Some were excellent plumbers early on.

And so it was that in 2013 I emerged from college with the complete NVQ2 plumbing and heating qualification. I could continue my studies with the advanced NVQ3 qualification, including gas work. So I grabbed it, and at the end of that summer enrolled back into another two years of study.

Chapter 6

My first plumbing job

"No-one will give you a job," one of my best friends had declared. "Never, never, never. They'll want a man."

For a while, I believed her. I assumed the industry was too sexist. I was also an adult learner. Even on minimum wage, I was much more expensive than a 16-year-old apprentice. Already, I had two major marks against me.

And I'd done my research. I'd heard stories about women struggling to find jobs in the construction industry. Some had given up the job search and had set up their own plumbing businesses, muddling through until they felt competent. Others had given up plumbing entirely, and had returned to their previous careers.

But I was instantly optimistic when three entry-level job vacancies with a local housing company were announced at my college. By then, I'd finished the initial two-year plumbing course, and had enrolled in the higher-level, NVQ3 course at Weymouth college.

Our tutors handed the advert to my group. I was grateful not just to be given the advert, but to even be acknowledged as one of the students. On the first day at college, a few weeks earlier, the tutor had thought I'd walked into the wrong classroom. He hadn't been expecting me.

"This is the plumbing Level 3 course," he'd barked, when I'd walked into the classroom. A whiteboard behind him showed a diagram of water supplies, from a pumping station through a town to people's homes. Cool, I thought. I'm in the right place. I took a seat, trying to blend in quietly.

"I said, this is plumbing," he repeated. "Where are you supposed to be?"

"Plumbing," I replied.

"What, Level 3?"

"Yes."

"Not Level 2?"

"No. I finished that last year. I'm on the Level 3 course."

He flicked his computer on, stared at it briefly, and then shrugged. He must have found me on the register. So I could stay. I sank into my seat, feeling self-conscious when I wanted to be invisible.

Though I didn't stay invisible for long. By lunchtime, I'd relaxed into the course. This was plumbing — something I loved, and what I wanted to be studying. And the other students seemed OK. By now, all the students were over 18 years old. Some had taken a study break of a year or two since the previous courses. They'd all grown up since the Level 2 group of 16-year-olds. Some were in long-term relationships. Some were parents.

There was also a small group of 'mature' students. There were four of us. None of us had plumbing jobs or apprenticeships. We'd formed an informal little group, and sat together and did practical work together. So in true pack mentality, we crowded around the job advert to find out more.

The company needed three plumber's mates to work on a four-year project involving switching homes from electric storage heaters to modern gas boilers and radiators.

A senior plumber would take charge of each home, and we'd assist with the easier plumbing and menial tasks.

It would be great experience, and a chance to build up our gas portfolios and to get our NVQ3 logbooks completed.

I was instantly excited and hopeful, and I applied for the job. A week later, I was summoned to an interview at the housing association's head office.

I asked my tutor what I should wear to such an interview. He looked at me like I'd farted. He often looked at me, and the other students in that way. Sometimes, he'd say we looked like stunned cows, staring at him. He could be a bit abrasive.

"What?" he barked.

"No matter."

I opted for a smart shirt and trousers, and tied my hair back.

First, my prospective employers led me to an empty conference room, where I was to sit a half-hour test to test my general plumbing knowledge. I worked my way through the paper. Some of the answers I knew, some I didn't. Could this be a problem? How high a score did I need?

I figured that plumbing was about using one's wits and creativity, and finding solutions to problems. This was a problem that could be easily solved. Having glanced around the room to see if there was a webcam pointed at me (I couldn't see one), I pulled out my phone and looked up the answers on Google. So far so good.

I quickly finished the paper, and glanced around. On the table was a pile of question papers. It got me thinking. How many people were being interviewed for this job? Had they printed out the exact number of test papers for each person? As I reached over, to flick through (and count them), the door swung open.

"Alright" asked the two men who entered.

I pulled my hand back, embarrassed that I'd been caught.

"Yes," I squeaked back, as I regained my composure. "I've finished the test."

I was ushered into a smaller office. One of the men was the manager. The other was the project foreman. They sat opposite me, and began the interview. First came the chit-chat. I'd lived in Australia. Tell us more. I'd been a journalist. I'd retrained. Why? We then discussed the plumbing job.

The job would, unfortunately, involve installing a lot of pipes. I was confused. What did they mean by "unfortunately"? Wasn't that good? I explained that I wanted to install pipes, and learn as much as possible about plumbing installations. They seemed pleased by my answer. After a few more general questions about my background and interests, the interview was over. I'd hear from them in a few days.

I wondered, did I have them over a barrel? They were looking for NVQ3 students, or equivalent. If they didn't take me on, but took male colleagues instead, would they have to justify why? I was, after all, a star student with an excellent college record. Plus I had basic hand tools, and my own car.

As promised, the letter arrived, saying they'd like to offer me a job. I was over the moon. This was the opportunity I'd been dreaming of. This would help set up my new career. Everything changed overnight, from uncertainty and struggle to proper mentoring and training.

Three weeks later, I turned up to my first day on-site. A uniform and work boots were waiting for me. A lengthy induction period of online courses was ahead of me. But for the moment, I'd be on the tools.

'The guys will love your pink backpack,' said the office staff, as they took the photo for my work pass, and waved me off. 'You'll get ribbed for that.'

So off I went, with my pink backpack. The work site was just outside Dorchester, which was ideal for me — only 20 minutes drive from my home in Weymouth. Other locations would be as far as an hour away. I'd have to make the journey in my own car, in my own time at my own expense, every day. My hours would be 8.30 am to 4.30pm daily, with one day a week spent at college.

That morning, I met my new colleagues. There were

six of us in the team — three experienced plumbers (the foreman from my interview, an experienced boiler repairer, and a former soldier turned gas engineer). And three plumbers mates — myself, another student from my course, and a general plumber/handyman.

They were interested to know about me. I liked them. They were friendly and chatty, and seemed like nice people. And they were also funny. It didn't take long for the banter to kick in. My rucksack was ignored. First my delicate hammer was laughed at — I hadn't realised it was so small. And then it was my dodgy parking that grabbed their mirth.

"Whose car is that?" one of them pointed. "Look how it is parked."

They all looked at my car — a scruffy, 10-year-old navy Ford Fusion, parked at a very slight angle to the curb. I thought it was parked just fine. "God, that is terrible parking," they remarked, as they wandered over to my car. "Isn't that your car, Jennie?"

My new bosses hadn't been allowed to ask about my family in the interview. My children's child seats were noticed in the backseat. The foreman peered in at them.

"So, you've got children? How many? What ages?" he asked. "Wait until they get ill. You'll be needing to go home to look after them."

"Nah," I said. "I won't. Will I?"

"Yes," he said. "You will. I've got a son. We've all got children. I know these things."

So, I was one parent among many. That seemed like a good start. And so began my first day of work. I hung my first, of probably hundreds of radiators, for them that morning. I'd hung them before. But the foreman showed me how he wanted them installed, before leaving me to do the rest.

Also that morning, I learned my first — literally painful — lesson. Be Careful Where You Put The Soldering Torch. I was barely an hour into the job. I'd soldered the first radiator connection. I'd turned the torch off, and had stood it behind me while I grabbed a cloth.

As I swiveled back round to my work, my wrist caught the top of the nozzle, which was still extremely hot. For a moment, I didn't feel anything. I thought I'd got away with it. But then, searing pain shot up my arm, and an angry red welt emerged on my skin.

I'd have run to put my wrist under a cold tap any other time. But I was too embarrassed. It was my first morning. My boss would think I was clumsy, accident-prone, and maybe even incompetent. It wouldn't look good. So I turned my watering eyes away from my companions, and suffered through the pain. My wrist throbbed for a couple of hours. And I'd be left with a small scar that would take a couple of years to vanish. But I managed to hide my misfortune.

Lunch came and went. We ate inside a community hall which was part of the complex. A resident handed me a key, giving me access to the resident communal toilets.

"You can't use the men's toilets," she insisted, referring to the plastic cabin in the car park. "That's just not nice for you."

So I thanked her, and took the key. And I used the special toilet for the ten weeks we were based there.

In the afternoon, the fun continued. Looking back, I wonder what my bosses and colleagues had expected of me. I'm a 5ft6, athletic but otherwise a typical woman in terms of physical strength.

But my physical strength didn't match that of my male colleagues. None of them had worked with a female plumber before. Management had instructed them to treat me as one of the lads. I was to do the same work and tasks as a man. I wasn't to be treated any differently.

Some furniture needed moving. It was in the way of where we wanted to run some pipes. As a plumbers' mate, my boss asked me to deal with it. I went into the living room, and was confronted by huge, mahogany display cabinet. It had already been emptied of its contents.

"Could you move it out of the way?" asked my boss, pointing across the room to where he'd like it to go. It didn't look too big or heavy. I could do this. Or so I thought.

"OK," I said. I squatted down, and tried to push it. Nothing happened. I pushed again — it didn't even move a centimetre. It was like it was glued to the floor.

"I need to eat more pies," I muttered. "Get some weight behind me."

"What?" said my boss.

I pushed again, but it still wouldn't move.

"Oh, get up," sighed my boss. "I'll get someone else to move it."

One of my colleagues, a strapping young man who was twice the size of all of us, was summoned. It slid along the floor for him. In the future, he'd always be called first for such tasks. And I was sent back to my radiators.

And that was my first day. Not all of it went smoothly. Nonetheless, I went home on a high. I was finally getting hands-on experience, and learning things about plumbing that you couldn't find in a textbook. And I was getting paid for it. And my colleagues seemed like a good bunch. What more could I ask for?

Chapter 7

You're strong – for a girl

Inga is strong. Inga is a weightlifter. Inga is stronger than anyone in this room. Inga is a woman. Inga is a Swedish bionic mass of blonde hair and rippling muscle that I'll never match up to. I hate Inga.

It was a Thursday morning — the first Thursday of the month, and the allocated time for my workplace's monthly department meeting. Our numbers included the plumbers, the kitchen fitters and the bathroom fitters. And our various managers. Around 20 of us sat on high-backed old-people armchairs in the community hall, munching on bacon rolls and sipping tea.

Besides the female admin assistant taking notes, I was the only woman in the room.

In front of us, our health and safety officer was giving a presentation on safe lifting techniques, and how to gauge our abilities. This included the description of Inga, a woman he had once met, and who wasn't to be messed with.

Official guidelines are that a man limits himself to a maximum lift of 25kg, and a woman 16kg — depending on how close to the body the weight is held, and how high or low it is to be lifted. *14

But these are just recommended guidelines. Throw in unique personal qualities, and maybe injury, age, genetics, etc, and that can vary. Which is what our speaker was saying.

"Be aware of what is a safe lifting weight for you," he said. "If you need help, ask for it. There's no need to struggle on your own."

And his parting nugget of wisdom: Don't underestimate a woman's physical strength. We were in an age of equality. One couldn't discriminate in terms of gender.

"Women can be just as strong as men," he finished.

No comment. My colleagues listened patiently and quietly. One of them gently snored — a sufferer of sleep apnoea, who struggled to stay awake if sat in a warm room/soft chair.

I glanced around the room. The men ranged in age from early 20s to late 50s. But I was pretty confident that they were all stronger than me. I wouldn't even be close to matching their strength. As women go, I'm pretty average in physical strength and fitness. I have some very strong female friends. One has taken up weight-lifting, and filmed herself lifting free weights of 80kg off the floor. She'd be great hoisting a boiler onto the wall.

But another friend doubts that women can be plumbers — despite knowing me, and the work that I do. Her father was a plumber. When she was growing up, they'd discuss the possibility of female plumbers. He felt it just wasn't possible. Women didn't have the brute strength.

I estimate that he would have been a plumber in the 1970s to 90s. Quite possibly, in those days it wasn't possible. After all, boilers were heavier than they are now — they had cast iron heat exchangers that I could barely lift off the floor. I use a sack tray to wheel these boilers out of the house, if they need to be removed.

Power tools weren't as good as they are today. I'm very fond of my angle grinder, and mini circular saw. And also my multi-tool (an electrical tool with a vibrating head, which can cut through wood and pipe, but not injure the human hand).

I also work mainly with copper pipe (rather than steel or lead). I have a nifty set of benders, which I use to shape the pipe. In days gone by, so my tutors told me, a plumber might bend the pipe over their knee, or around a tree. I also carry a sack tray, and a trolley, in the van. And I have a lightweight 'concertina' ladder to access attics. These are just a few of the developments in the industry which have worked in women's favour.

Another non-plumber friend doubted that I'd be able to undo rusted nuts and fittings. As it happened, this wouldn't be a particular issue for me. If a fitting is tight, a longer-handled tool generally gives me the torque to undo it. If it still won't turn, maybe some lubricating oil can help? Perhaps some heat from a soldering torch to expand the joint?

Sometimes, more specialised tools can help. For example, some tap connections can be very tight to undo, especially if they've rusted. The tight access to some connections doesn't help.

But this was less of an issue after I invested in a top-quality tap-removal kit.

Some issues aren't more of a problem for female plumbers. They're just part of the job. But the tools help provide other solutions to the challenges.

But one shouldn't overlook the fact that this is an extremely physical job, which places a lot of demands on both male and female bodies. I know of men who have suffered injuries, and had to give up the tools — one of them went into teaching. Another works in a plumber's merchant.

I didn't want to hurt myself. If I was at a physical disadvantage, by being female, I wanted to know more. I wanted to know how I was weaker, what issues may arise from this, and how I could work round such problems. So I went online.

Fact 1. Women have half the strength of men in their upper bodies, and two-thirds of their strength in their lower bodies. Squats and lunges come easier to women than press-ups. *15

Fact 2. A woman's body has about 30 to 35 percent muscle by weight. A man's body has 40 to 50 percent muscle — depending on age, fitness levels and genetics. *16

Fact 3. Men are generally taller and bigger than women, and tend to be faster at sprinting, jumping and swimming. However, when you consider the proportional difference in height and muscle area, women are stronger in their events. *17

Fact 4. Many flexibility-related movements, such as yoga and stretching, are more challenging for men. *18

Fact 5. Women can sometimes outlast men in endurance sports like long-distance trail running. This is thought to be because women burn more fat, and less carbohydrate, during such activities. In 2002, a 35-year-old woman called Jasmin Paris won the 146-mile Badwater ulta-marathon, beating more than 100 men. The next person — and fastest man — finished 15 hours behind her. *19

In my younger days, I sometimes beat my male competitors in races. First was the ski race, which came at the end of a week-long beginner's ski holiday in Italy. A mini slalom had been set up, on one of the nursery slopes. We were each timed to see how fast we could get down it.

My competitive buttons had been pressed. I didn't put the breaks on. It was a hair-raising journey down the slope, and I only just managed to stay upright. But I got down in the shortest time. And in the apres ski bar that night, I took top place on the winner's podium and was awarded a medal — which I still have today.

The fact that a female had won gained some amusement from students and instructors alike. The guys I had beaten thought it funny. I was also accused of being a 'reckless nutter' by my friends, which was a fair comment.

Another time, also in my early 20s, I was in a backpacker hostel in Israel when I participated in a game of tag rugby. Roughly equal numbers of men and women took part. The idea wasn't to beat each other up — it was a game of tag. The guy I'd been dating was also taking part, and was trying to catch me as I sprinted up the pitch. I knew someone was on my tail, but I didn't look to see who. I just ran faster. And being a keen cross-country runner at the time, I could shift.

And so — to the amusement of everyone on the pitch — I outran my boyfriend. He couldn't catch me. Later, when we discussed the game, he accused me of doing it on purpose.

"Isn't that the aim of the game?" I'd asked. "I'm not supposed to let you catch me."

"That's not what I'm saying," he'd whinged. "You did it to humiliate me. You shouldn't have done it."

Not long after that, we went our separate ways.

Another time, I beat a male friend in a swimming race. We were at our local pool, and had a lane to ourselves. I'd been training for an outdoor swimming race at the time, so I was pretty fit. So I accepted when he challenged me to a two-lap race (of about 50m).

A count of three, and we were off. From the outset, we both swam hard. It wasn't going to be an easy race for either of us. But I ended up winning — albeit only just. But I was the clear winner.

'You certainly know how to make a guy feel good,' he remarked.

Some of my female friends have also out-shone their male companions, which hasn't been taken well by the men. One of my friends is a super-fit and very keen cyclist. She often goes on challenging group rides, which take her on long distances up steep terrain. On one ride, she was the first rider to reach the summit. Her male companions couldn't keep up with her.

Most of the group took this in good spirits, and were proud to have such a talented woman in their midst. But one guy didn't take it well, and similarly accused her of beating him on purpose, with the sole goal of humiliating him.

One can't help but wonder why some men are so upset to be outdone by female competitors. Women aren't to be overlooked, or underestimated. Women can achieve amazing things.

I'm not a super-athlete. As I get older, I'm becoming less of an athlete and am starting to suffer more aches and pains that typically follow one through her 40s and beyond. But despite this, I can undoubtedly maximise my physical talents. I decided to make the most of what I had, as I'd seen other female plumbers do.

During my early days of plumber training, I spent a couple of days of work experience with a female plumber in the next town. As part of a bathroom renovation, she needed to remove an old, steel pipe that was screwed tight into its 30-year-old socket.

She was a fit, young woman who used to be in the armed forces. But the joint was stuck tight, so she needed as much torque as possible to unscrew it. Her solution: she slid an old metal bar onto her wrench to get more leverage. And she then sat on the floor, put her feet on the wall and used her leg muscles to push the joint apart. And she managed it. Her apprentice watched on, proudly.

"Isn't she amazing,"'she said. "She knows which muscles to use, to get the most strength."

And I saw that while I didn't have the upper body strength of the average man, I did have powerful muscles. The trick was to use my body intelligently, like I'd just seen this woman do.

I started attending exercise classes to build core muscles — press ups, sit-ups and planks. I also got fitter and stronger through work. I have little arm muscles. I was lucky I looked good with the muscles — I became toned and athletic, and lost a bit of tummy flab. I'd worried I'd look butch and unfeminine. But quite the opposite happened. I thought I looked good. Rob still seemed to find me attractive, even when I flexed my baby biceps at him.

One evening, he struggled to unscrew the lid on the pickled onions. He's much bigger than me, and stronger than me. Albeit a little out of shape, he is a bit of a hunk. But anyway, in jest, I told him to pass me the jar. I flicked it open with little effort. And then I almost wet myself by laughing.

But back at work, as the sole woman in an otherwise all-male group of plumbers, I wasn't the first choice of candidate to help move furniture, or other heavy lifting. Initially, my colleagues had intended to treat me just like the guys. This would include the same lifting demands. But in reality, it wasn't my forte — if you'll accept the pun.

However, we were a team. We all had unique qualities to bring to our jobs. I was still a trainee plumber, confined to pipe runs and hanging radiators. But there were a lot of radiators and pipes to be installed, which kept me busy. Another team member had physical strength, and could also plaster walls. Another was an experienced boiler repairer, and could diagnose faults. Another thought nothing of scaling ladders. We were all different, and all valuable in our own ways. And we all liked working together, and enjoyed each others company. Which made us a brilliant team.

But the talk about Inga got me thinking… what were my limits? What could I achieve? Plumbing is a very physical job, so how would my physical limitations shape my future career?

I discussed this with my colleagues. Of particular interest was how I would hang a boiler on the wall. It's all very well being able to fit the pipes and having the technical expertise to design the system. But I'd be a bit stuck if I couldn't get the boiler on the wall.

The boilers we installed were made by Vaillant. They were combi boilers (i.e., they heated hot water on demand — no need for a hot water cylinder or attic tanks). Some higher-powered boilers can weigh more than 40kg — well above the advised lifting limits for men or women.

The installation instructions say they are a two-person lift. But in real life, we fitted most of our boilers into airing cupboards. It was a squeeze for just one person to get in with a boiler. No way would a second person fit in there as well.

So my colleagues generally lifted the boilers onto the walls alone. Sometimes, if they had to use a step ladder, I'd spot them from behind — so they didn't lose their balance. But otherwise, it was a one-person lift.

This might be something my colleagues could manage now and again. But the dangers of doing this week in, week out wasn't lost on me. Such as the triple hernia that my boss was suffering, having done this work for 30-odd years. But still, I wanted to challenge myself. I wanted to know what I could achieve.

One morning, with some reluctance, two of my colleagues stood on either side of me as I lifted a boiler off the floor. They were worried that I could hurt myself, and also drop the boiler — an expensive piece of kit, costing hundreds of pounds.

"What do I do if you fall?" they asked. "How do we catch you, without our hands accidentally grabbing you, and going where they shouldn't?"

"You're my friends," I said. "If you have to, just catch me any way you have to. I want to try this."

First I squatted next to the boiler, and reached my arms around it. As I inched my hands underneath, I hugged the boiler, and hoisted it up onto one knee, and then against my chest — as I stood up. And what next? I stood there, cuddling the boiler. Yes, it was heavy. But I was OK. I was doing it.

"Right, great, you can put it down now," said my colleagues. So I lowered myself back down, put it back on my knee, and then onto the floor.

They hadn't had to catch me. I'd done this. Granted, it wasn't the quite the same challenge as lifting it onto the wall. But I'd lifted it off the floor. That was a start.

That was my first time lifting a boiler. It wasn't until a couple of years later, when I'd started plumbing alone, that I had to hang a boiler alone — and came across a difficult lift.

My first solitary boiler installations hadn't been too demanding. One was above a kitchen worktop, so I had a handy platform to work from — I lifted the boiler onto the worktop, hopped up myself, got up on one knee and used my strong thigh muscles to slide it up the wall.

But a more challenging install had come along. It was to be hung in the kitchen cupboard. The bottom of the boiler would be about level with my chin, and the bracket (for it to be hung on) higher than my head level. I had a step ladder to give me the height. But what about the weight? I knew it would be heavy. I took some advice on the matter. I chose another female plumber, herself an experienced plumber.

'You'll be just fine,' my advisor had said. 'You're stronger than you think Jennie. Have some faith in yourself.'

So, off I went. I got the old boiler off the wall fairly easily — first I stripped out the heavy components, so was left with the shell to pull down. And then up with the new one. It was heavy. Really heavy.

The best technique is to face the wall with the boiler in your arms, and to put the back of the boiler against the wall. You then slide the boiler up the wall and onto the bracket (the back of the boiler has a tab, which clicks onto the bracket). The longer you hang around, the quicker your arms tire. The lift needs to be done relatively quickly.

As I pushed the boiler up the wall, I seriously wondered if I could push it up. It was somewhat borderline, to say the least. I pushed it up the wall — almost there. But not quite. My arms started to shake. I took a deep breath, and tightened my stomach muscles. And I pushed again, hard and with all my might. The boiler clicked into place on the bracket. I'd been lucky, on this occasion. I treated myself to a tea break, and carried on with my work.

Not long after, another boiler install also nearly beat me. It was a like-for-like replacement of a combi boiler, in a utility room above a worktop. It seemed easy enough, so I got stuck in. After draining down the heating system, and disconnecting the various plumbing pipes, flue and electrics, I started to strip the boiler down.

First out was the heavy expansion vessel — a metal box about the same shape/size as a laptop bag, filled with a rubber 'balloon' and sometimes water. Great. That was the equivalent of a bag of sand gone. Out also came the pump. Another few kilograms gone. I hoisted the boiler off the wall, and lowered it onto the worktop. No issues so far.

It wasn't until I tried to carry it into the garden that I realised I'd over-stretched myself. The boiler still had some water in it — I hadn't completely drained it. It was super heavy. I almost fell over backwards as I scooped it into my arms. I only just managed to steady myself. And then carry it outside and drop it onto the lawn.

On both occasions, I could have been badly hurt if I'd fallen under the weight of the boilers. Or I could have damaged the boiler or the customer's property. The issue of lifting boilers onto walls couldn't be easily swept aside with an 'I'll be fine' flash of confidence. A strategy was needed.

Most customers didn't want me to do the heavy lifting. Often, (if male and in good health) they'd insist on helping me. But I had mixed feelings about this. Surely, as a professional plumber charging for professional work, I should be doing the lifting myself. Was it a cop-out to let the customer get hands-on? Could there be an insurance issue, if they got injured?

But it was also so easy to let them help. Sometimes, it seemed churlish not to — especially, on one occasion, when a father and adult son carried the new boiler up the stairs and, under my instructions, lifted it into position on the wall. Because even though I could have hung it myself, I would have struggled.

Regardless, I'd need safer lifting techniques for the future. So I looked at the installs that had worked well for me — i.e., lifting the boiler onto a worktop or portable workbench, then clambering up and hoisting it on my thigh. That technique seemed pretty reliable. Or, if it wasn't too high off the ground, I found that I could partially rest it on the top of my step ladder, while I composed myself for the lift.

And if I really couldn't hang it alone — such as on an install in a community centre kitchen, where the boiler was pretty high up, above a tiny worktop — I would pay a couple of guys to pop down for half an hour, to put it up for me.

So what had once seemed like a huge obstacle had solutions. I could find my own techniques to lift the boiler, or get someone to help me. I didn't have to do it alone. But my work would be easier if I was in peak fitness.

So I continued to do my weekly fitness regimen with a selection of YouTube videos. Bums and tums, and pilates, helped me build my core muscles. Zumba (dance fitness) helped with general fitness. And yoga helped with flexibility, and tight muscles.

As needs arose, I sometimes had to attend to smaller, lesser-used muscles.

During the pandemic lockdowns, I had trouble with my wrists. After playing swing-ball with my daughter, a particularly enthusiastic game left me with a sore wrist on my right arm.

Thankfully, I controlled the symptoms enough to continue working, initially with painkillers, and then with a compression bandage (which helped support my muscles). It took several weeks to heal fully.

Just in time for me to end up with a similar injury on the other wrist, I brought about during a toilet repair. I'd been lowering the cistern back onto the pan, when I felt an ache in my wrist. Initially, it seemed to heal. But then the pain returned, to the point that I could barely pick up a cup of tea with my left hand, and that it was a strain to play my guitar — let alone do a plumbing compression joint up. That injury also took several weeks to heal.

These physical limitations and injuries are just some of many problems that I've had to solve as a plumber.

They show that even seemingly small injuries can make physical work difficult.

Chapter 8

Mixed messages

"Just don't get your hopes up." My six-month probation period at my housing company job had almost expired. It hadn't been a good day. I'd been working alone with the foreman, and some of my pipework had been messy. This was one of his bugbears. He took great pride in tidy pipework. It was a work of art, and a sign of a good craftsman. My offering was awful.

"You can't leave it like that," he d barked. "Take it out, and start again, and do it properly."

He was right. I was six months in, and I should have known better. In general, my work was pretty tidy. But I seemed to have hit an afternoon glitch, like I'd been working blindfolded. But what did he mean by "don't get your hopes up."

The previous months had flown by in a blur of pipes and soldering. So many radiators had been hung. So many holes drilled, and joists notched. I'd learned so much — things that one could never glean from a textbook, such as how to drill through angled architrave on a ceiling or use a circular saw without it kicking back.

Every day was interesting. The radio would go on, and we'd settle into the cycle of work, tea break, banter, work, lunch, more banter. Each day would fly by. I loved my job.

By now, we were down to two plumbers' mates. One of my colleagues had fallen at the three-month probation.

He'd been too friendly with a customer's teenage daughter. He'd been warned off, by both parents and our boss. But to no avail — he wasn't good at following instructions. He was already unpopular with the senior plumbers, and had a reputation as a know-it-all who came out with rubbish suggestions. Even though I counted him as a friend, I didn't like working with him either.

But my employer had a reputation and a duty of care to uphold. The issue of befriending underage customers was questionable. Rather than deal with the difficulties of firing him due to misconduct, the failed three-month probation was the easiest way to get rid of him. It happened quickly, and quietly. One day he was on site. The next, he wasn't. So we were now one man down, with the foreman working alone.

No complaints had come my way about my work or conduct. So I thought I was doing well. So the comment from my boss that day confused me.

I thought back, over the last few months. I was a beginner, and mistakes had been made. But nothing serious — pipes run perhaps a little less than parallel, the odd leak, and a radiator hung in the way of a door shutting. But as time went on, these issues were getting ironed out.

I'd been paired with an experienced, 50-year-old boiler engineer — a chilled-out bloke, full of anecdotes and a love of reggae and skittles.

One of his favourite sayings was 'It's illegal to struggle.' And so, all our jobs seemed easy. We worked in a relaxed manner, taking our time over things. But we got through the work faster than the other teams. He knew what he was doing, and things would be done the best way from the outset.

He taught me loads of practical skills. But the biggest lesson I learned was to 'go slow, go fast', which meant taking one's time getting the initial planning and preparation ready and not rushing (as mistakes are made when one rushes). If something is difficult, one should pause for a moment. Take a break, and look for the best way ahead.

Our work was highly rated. We had nothing but positive feedback from the customers, whose houses we'd worked in. They loved their new heating systems, and they'd also loved having us working in their homes.

Many times, the customers regarded us as almost bosom-buddies, in barely a couple of hours. So many times, life secrets and confessions would be shared, as I was on my knees hooking up radiators. I'd nod politely and respond appropriately while doing my work. And they'd carry on chatting. And then my colleague might come into the room for a bit, so they'd repeat all their secrets to him.

They were also fascinated in me, as the sole, female plumber on the team. Most of them had never seen a woman doing this kind of work before, and they watched me with interest. Many of them asked how I'd ended up in this job, and why I'd wanted to be a plumber.

I was fawned over, much to the amusement and annoyance of my colleagues. Yes, the adoration would never have been dished out to a man, and it was condescending and patronising. Things were said to me that you couldn't imagine being said to a man.

Let's switch the comments around. Could you imagine a man being told:

"Aren't you a clever boy?"

"How did you learn to do all this?

"Did your mum teach you?"

"You're too handsome to be doing this job."

One of the funniest interchanges came a few years later, after I'd qualified as a gas engineer, and was out working on my own. I was in a block of sheltered accommodation for older people, in the midst of a boiler service. I'd nipped outside, to take measurements from a gas meter when I heard voices behind me. It was two old ladies, who were interested in my work.

"I'm a gas engineer," I explained, and said I was working on the boiler in the flat behind us.

"Really?" said one of them. "I had no idea. I thought you were just taking meter readings."

Her friend chastised her, pointing out that women did all sorts of jobs in the modern age, and that she shouldn't make comments like that. But she wouldn't be silenced.

"Aren't you a clever girl," she added. She just had to say it, as they all do.

And it seems I wasn't just clever. I was pretty too. At one house, the elderly couple seemed very excited by my looks. The lady gasped when she clapped eyes on me, and ran to fetch her husband.

"Come and see how pretty she is," she marvelled. "She's too pretty to be a plumber."

I didn't feel very pretty, with my messy hair and work clothes, but it seems my gorgeousness shone through — on that day, anyway.

For ages, I tried to hide my femininity at work. I thought that by dressing as a man, I'd better blend into the male workforce. This is the approach I took at my first job, for the housing company. But this wasn't the case at all. I looked like the woman I was, dressed in a t-shirt and work trousers.

Though I did manage, on one occasion, to fool a dog belonging to one of the customers. Because their dog didn't like women (other than the wife or grown-up daughter who'd sometimes visit), the customer had recommended a male plumber be assigned to their house.

This information was relayed to me as I waited with my colleagues to be let into the customer's house. Admittedly I'm not much of a dog person, but like most people I'm somewhat unsettled if one starts growling at me.

So in we went. I huddled in the middle of the group. And all eyes settled on the dog — an Alsation. It looked us up and down, sniffed around, and then pottered off. Not much drama there. When we left the house a few minutes later, and were safely back outside, the foreman burst out laughing at me.

'It thought you were a man,' he chortled. And then he started laughing so hard, he was bent double.

I just quietly took his mirth. I thought he'd been out of order to put me in that position. But no harm was done. I wasn't assigned that house, so I wouldn't be going back. I wasn't about to make an issue over it.

On another occasion, I was due to work in a flat where the neighbour had an issue with women.

It seemed just the sight of a woman would unsettle him, and — if a woman got too close — he'd start to cry. I accidentally met him when I popped out to the van to grab some tools. He was an older man, in a wheelchair, and was having trouble getting his keys in the door.

"Let me help you," I said.

I darted over, unlocked the door for him and pushed it open. He started to cry.

"Oh no, are you OK?" I asked.

As I tried to comfort him, he cried more. At this point, his carer came around the corner and took over. And he explained the problem to me.

So, aside from the dog, pretty much everyone was aware of my femininity, as they'd often point it out to me. And in the early days, at the housing company, this would annoy my male colleagues, who thought the favourable attention due to my gender was unfair. And they were right, it wasn't fair. And yes, I lapped it up and I loved it.

'Why, thank you,' I'd reply to the customers, when they commented on my cleverness. And then, to my colleagues: "Did you hear that? She said I'm 'awesome."

And they'd usually find a humorous quip to relay back. Banter was an integral part of our existence. We'd chat a lot while working, about our home lives, families and partners, finances, holidays, hopes and dreams. And at other times, we'd tease each other. It was like a game of tennis. The banter would go back and forth. Most of the team members entered into it quite merrily. Sometimes, it could get quite boisterous when the foreman wasn't around.

One occasion, a colleague accused me of being fat as I squeezed through an attic hatch. My shirt had pulled up slightly, and a bit of tummy was exposed. I responded by chucking a pipe clip at him. My aim wasn't that great. I aimed a metre or so to the right. I didn't mean it to hit him, but the clip hit him on the head. Luckily he took it in good humour.

One of our favourite topics was a 'battle of the sexes', in which we'd debate the pros and cons of the other's gender. My nugget of wisdom, one day, was that I wasn't surprised that men didn't like going to the doctors. Why? They all asked. Because they make you drop your pants and bend over, or so I've heard.

It was all silly stuff, and good-natured. We just all wanted to have a giggle as we worked.

Another time, we got onto the topic of yoga. Some of the guys considered themselves very fit and athletic, and physically able.

So they rose to a lunchtime challenge of doing a yogic 'crow' pose in our lunch room. The pose involves squatting, like a cat — with your hands on the ground before you. And then you lean forwards, wrap your knees around your elbows, and pull your feet up off the ground. It's not easy to do — it takes some practice. So that kept us amused one lunchtime.

On another occasion, I blurted out a comeback to my boss — something none of us would generally dare to even think of doing. Three of us (him, myself and another plumber) were laying pipework. It was a Friday afternoon. The other two guys had done their bits, and were waiting for me to finish.

"If you were a man, it would have been done by now," our boss remarked.

"No," I said. "If I were a man, it would be done tomorrow."

"Jennieeee," gasped the other plumber's mate. "You can't say that."

But regardless, I put my tools down and laughed. And thankfully, our boss also saw the funny side of my remark and laughed. And I finished my work in high spirits. It was one of my best off-the-cuff comebacks. What my boss said was a sexist, unkind remark that would have made HR cringe. But I batted it straight back, defusing a situation that could have upset me and made me feel bad.

Humour helped me through the job, and helped me get along with my colleagues. The banter helped cement us as a team and smooth the way when our boss was around.

And so the weeks turned into months. Summer turned to autumn. And I continued to learn the precious skills, that would come in so handy for my blossoming career.

My boss had high standards, which was a mixed blessing. He pushed me to take pride in my work, and to work to a professional standard with plumbing that I could be proud of. Several years later, he is still in my thoughts when I'm pulling bends on pipes, and similar.

But while he was a fantastic plumber, and great at organising and overseeing our work, he could be highly critical and sharp with his words. All of us dreaded working with him. I seemed to muddle along OK with him, on the odd occasion that I was put on a job with him. Or at least, we got on OK until my probation period was up. Out of the blue, he said "Just don't get your hopes up."

"What?"

He said that he didn't want me to be kept on. The day before, he'd attended a meeting with the manager, to discuss my short-comings. His words were: "It's not that we don't like you. But… well, just don't get your hopes up."

I pushed for more details. But he regretted saying what he had. He said that he shouldn't have said anything. I'd have to wait until my probation meeting with our manager, the following week, to find out more.

It was the end of a long week of working alone with him, in an empty three-bedroom house about 40 minutes away from my home. I'd been trying all week to impress him, but hadn't succeeded. I was exhausted.

The frustration was too much for me. I stomped off to my car to pack my tools away, and burst into tears. I managed to regain my composure, only to bump into him outside the property. I burst into tears again, and then tried to deny my distress. Yes, I knew I looked upset. I was, after all, sobbing. But I tried to claim I was just tired, which was obviously not true. I then drove home mortified.

The following week, I started work in a new property, back with my usual colleagues. The previous Friday afternoon felt surreal — did the boss really tell me my job was on the line? Had I really burst into tears?

That afternoon, our manager visited me at work. He called 'hello' and poked his head up through the loft hatch. How did he know I was there? I thought I was in a hidey-hole — tucked away like an animal in its den. But there he was, looking his usual cheerful, happy self.

He got straight to the point. My six-month probation had come up, and he was pleased to offer me a permanent job. I was being kept on.

"The job is yours, if you want it," he said.

There was no feedback over my inadequacies. Just forms to fill in, which I signed on the spot. And then he was off, and I was alone again. Just me, in the attic, with my pipes and soldering kit.

Chapter 9

The good, the bad and being female

"How are you going to make all your lost hours up?" demanded my boss.

I'd been trying to avoid him all morning, but I had just crossed paths with him outside a customer's front door. I'd only nipped out to retrieve a tool from a colleague.

"You owe us back for all those trips to the dentist, and all those times you had to pick up your sick children from school," he continued. "It all adds up. That's lost time for the company."

Standing outside a customer's property, and having this conversation — albeit unplanned — felt unprofessional. Though such was the nature of our workplace, we didn't have an office to retreat to.

My boss was crabby. He was often in a bad mood. None of us knew why. Some of the guys reckoned he needed 'female company'. I reckoned he needed to smoke some weed. But either way, he was a difficult individual to read — one could never tell his mood by looking at him. But one became aware of it when it was directed at you.

It felt like a lover's tiff, to argue with a bloke outside a house. And now I was frustrated too. I'd been working with him for about a year, and he'd never said anything about wanting the time back. And I hadn't heard any such requests that my colleagues make up for their lost time.

Typically, everyone on the team needed the odd

hour out here or there. One of my colleagues was in the process of buying a house and needed to go to house viewings. Another had had to collect his young daughter from school a few times. And everyone had had the occasional dentist or medical appointment. One guy had needed a planned operation, and was told to book it in as 'sick leave'.

Was I being singled out? It certainly felt so. He'd obviously been stewing over this for some time. And now the resentment was flooding out of him.

"How are you going to give us the time back?" he demanded, again.

He hadn't come up with any suggestions. It wasn't as though I could take my work home and catch up with it in the evenings. Overtime wasn't an option either, as — aside from my childcare obligations — the customers would want their homes to themselves in the evenings and early mornings.

"Umm, do you want me to work through a couple of break-times and lunchtimes?" I suggested.

"You can't do that. You have to have breaks by law. And you're no good to us if you're tired."

So where did he think we were going with this conversation? I'd been surprised — I'd had no idea it was an issue. As long as absences were only very occasional, and only for an hour or two, and for exceptional circumstances, it had seemed to be accepted. And I'd thought myself lucky to have an employer who gave us that flexibility. And, in return, we'd be loyal, hard-working and devoted plumbers who would give our best to our jobs.

How naive had I been? However, I did have one solution. How about I sacrifice a day's annual leave and come in to work that day? A day should easily cover my accumulated time off the tools.

"That's a bit extreme," he said. "Are you sure you want to do that?"

But I couldn't think of any other solutions. And he

didn't discount the suggestion. So off we returned to our various jobs, leaving it at that.

But it got me thinking. When my male colleagues were called upon for family duties, there was a sense of admiration — they were responsible, reliable family men who were an asset to their communities. These were guys you could call upon in your hour of need. Meanwhile, I felt like a liability. When I was called away from the tools, it was a sign that I wasn't 100 percent committed to the job. Other things, such as my children, came first.

When did you hear 'Oh, you're such a great mother, for pitching in with the childcare drop-offs, dental appointments, and bath times'? With this realisation, other things started to make sense.

At the time, I was still attending college one day a week, to complete my plumbing training. This higher-level course also included gas engineering, and would lead to certification as a Gas Safe registered engineer.

Back at work, I'd been collecting evidence of jobs for my college logbook. And my bosses and colleagues had all been super supportive. I'd compiled lots of tasks, lots of write-ups and was making great progress. I'd even spent mornings with other plumbing teams (such as the repairs team) to tick off my various tasks. My bosses did everything they could to help me through my college course.

Yet at the same time, I was reminded that this was a temporary (four-year) role. Once the project was over, I might not have a job. I should look at my job as a springboard to get skills and experience to take me to greater heights with a different employer.

Fair enough, I thought. At least they are honest with me, and I could plan accordingly. But almost in the same breath, they asked my colleague if he'd like to train as a gas engineer. This would involve a promotion so that he could take charge of some of the boiler installations.

It would be a great opportunity, they told him. They'd pay for his training. They'd provide him with all the onsite experience. He'd earn more money, which would set his family up nicely. He'd be an idiot not to grab the opportunity. But my colleague graciously declined — he didn't fancy all the studying. He was more of a hands-on guy — his first trade was building/plastering. He liked to be hands-on with his jobs, rather than stuck in manuals and gas calculations.

The company only had the funds to train one person, and they'd chosen him. But when he didn't accept, they didn't ask me. I was paying for my college fees. I still had several months of study ahead of me, but I could be fast-tracked through — with their support. I didn't understand why they didn't offer me the opportunity.

Or it least, at the time I didn't understand. Now, perhaps I do. I wasn't valued in the same way as my colleague. If I were, I'd also have been funded for gas training. We were both hard-working, diligent, conscientious, and personable, and — by then — competent in our roles as plumbers mates. We both had a lot of potential, and a lot to offer the company.

When he declined their offer, the bosses decided to advertise externally for another, already qualified, gas engineer to join our team.

"We need someone now," they'd said, seemingly forgetting about their plans to train my colleague. "We can't wait for you to qualify, Jennie."

So I was overlooked as a candidate.

Let's look at gender equality for a bit. Gender equality is equal access to resources and opportunities regardless of gender. This means not being discriminated in the workplace, due to one's gender.

This is all great in theory. And my company had very clear equal opportunity policies — both for staff and customers. But in practice, and despite best intentions, gender equality can be a difficult ideal to navigate. How is one to know if you are overlooked because of gender? If I was a bloke, would my prospects have been different?

Or would the outcome have been the same? How could I possibly know?

There's also confusion as to what gender equality is. According to a cartoon doing the rounds on social media, it's not equality we should strive for, but equity. Equality is equal treatment. But equity recognises that the starting position might differ for certain groups of people, and so sees a need for targeted support (aka special treatment) to bring everyone to a common place.

The cartoon shows three people watching a sports match. They aren't in the grounds. Instead, they're trying to peer over the perimeter fence. One person is very tall, and can easily see over the fence. But neither the medium or short person can see over it. How do you level it up so everyone has the same view?

The solutions are shown in the cartoon. Example 1 is equality. Each is given a small, identical box to stand on. As expected, the tall person has an even higher vantage. This time, the medium person can just about see over. But the short person still needs to be higher.

Which is where example 2 comes to the rescue. Example 2 is equity. The tall person gives their box to the short person, who is now elevated by two boxes. This time, all three heads are at the same vantage, and everyone can see over the fence.

Equity is the key. Treating people with different needs and circumstances in the same way won't always bring them up to the same place. So many times, I've been told 'We can't have one rule for the men, and another for the women. They'd never accept that.'

But why shouldn't they? And this need not just be limited to gender. It could be ethnicity, disabilities, age, etc. Let's jump ship for a moment, and look at age.

As is the case with gender, it is illegal to discriminate in terms of age. The aim is to protect access to jobs and opportunities for all ages. Yet there's been a flip-side. If equality has been taken to treating everyone equally, then older people are expected to match their younger, and often fitter, colleagues in terms of work output and performance. All great if you work in an office, but what about if you have a practical, physically demanding job?

I got talking to an older friend in the gym about this. Her husband works in a garage. He's been a mechanic all his working life, though now — in his 60s — he feels the physical demands of his work. He can't afford to retire. Yet his employer expects the same work from him as the lads in their 20s.

Another tradesman I know is still expected to carry, and climb, high ladders up to his retirement age of 65. Sometimes, he could be working atop these ladders for an hour at a time. Sometimes longer.

Years ago, his employer (a big national company) forbade ladder climbing beyond the age of 55. Other duties would be assigned to older workers, recognising that this is a dangerous and exhausting task that becomes harder with age. But not anymore.

Now aged 63, with bad knees and a weight problem, this man still climbs the ladders — a task he struggles with. And his bosses urge him to match the work output of his much-younger peers. Some of his colleagues are former soldiers, and he's unable to keep up with them. Yet because he has a mortgage to pay, and a family to support, he can't afford to give up his job.

"It's happening everywhere," my gym friend says. "A lot of my friends' husbands are under the same pressures. I think that, in the future, we're going to see a lot more work-related injuries. People will be working themselves to death."

I imagine the employers bleating, "If we let him go slow, won't they all demand to work slow? We can't have one rule for the old, and one for the young. And besides, we can't discriminate in terms of age.'"

What happened to teamwork, with colleagues pulling together and supporting each other? For while one colleague might be slower than another, they might have more experience, or be able to contribute more in another area. Staff shouldn't be set apart in such stark criteria.

In my case, maybe I needed a little more time off the tools than my male colleagues. Or maybe I hadn't needed any more time off, and it was just my boss's perception. Who's to know? But in a close-knit supportive team, one would hope there would be flexibility to account for such things. But due to this 'all or nothing' thinking, I've seen wasted talent from all sorts of people.

One woman I know — a brilliant nurse — suffered health issues that left her unable to work full-time. She didn't have the physical energy for it. She still wanted to work, but her employer refused part-time hours. As a result they lost a very talented staff member.

And other career women I know have seen their careers plateau after becoming mothers.

One of my best friends is one of them. After gaining a degree in psychology, she took a job as a civil servant. Her job was to analyse staff training and crime trends. And by all accounts, she was great at it. When her children were born, she dropped down to part-time hours so she could support the home front while her higher-earning husband could work longer hours in his career.

"Someone needed to feed the kids, and pick them up from school," she said. "And I wanted to do it. I wanted to look after my children, and progress in my career. But I wasn't able to do both."

To her dismay, her career plateaued. It's called being on a 'mummy track'. No promotion. No training opportunities. In her case, such opportunities weren't on offer for part-time workers. Maybe, she was told, if she returned full-time she could be considered. But those were the rules. Take it or leave it.

She spent the best part of ten years treading the same ground in her job, despite having so much more to offer. Eventually she took back control of her career, and embarked on a PhD-level course in counselling. When she's finished, she'll be one of the highest-qualified counsellors you can get. And she's planning to specialise in mothers. She's found a way forwards. But she's had to do it independently of her (part-time) day job.

Meanwhile, back in my job, I was again in trouble with the boss. My missed hours were — yet again — of concern. We'd started at a new job site, which was an hour's drive from my home. And my work hours, as always, began at 8.30am. But the earliest childcare available to me didn't start until 7.45am. I had no chance of getting to work on time. I didn't have any family or friends who could help out. The children's father was living an hour away himself, so he couldn't help. I was a bit stuck.

Luckily, the creche stayed open until 6pm, which gave me just enough time to get back to pick them up. Luckily they enjoyed being in childcare – they loved the various cooking/craft activities and toys, and outdoor play sessions. But it was a long day for them, which they did every day.

With the new worksite, each morning became a race. Me and the children would be waiting outside the creche, ready to dash through the doors when it opened so that I could begin my mad dash to work.

For the first few days at the new site, I arrived 20 minutes late every day. Sometimes later — such as when I got stuck behind a tractor on a country lane. But because our teams were scattered around the estate, initially, I managed to sneak in without being spotted by the foreman. Much as he'd like to, he couldn't monitor us all at once. One of my colleagues knew about my predicament.

"You'd better watch you're not caught," he mumbled.

But we were due to be there for six weeks, and I couldn't keep my lateness hidden for long.

At the end of the first week, the boss spotted me driving onto the estate. Later that day, he brought up the issue with me. I explained my problem, and said that

I didn't know what to do. But he wasn't interested in my problems. Why should he be? He reminded me that my work day began at 8.30am, and that I needed to be at work on time.

And so again I entered the fun place where the demands of being a mother clash with those of the workplace. You never quite meet the needs of either. Yet the pressure to successfully juggle the two is immense.

Three months earlier, it had been Christmas. I'd been given a 'super-mum' calendar for Christmas, by a family friend. She'd meant well. She was in awe of me and how much I achieved in both my work life and family life. But I didn't want to be a super-mum. I was exhausted and overwhelmed by my life. I wanted to have super-friends and super-support around me. Treating me as a super-mum was a cop-out for society.

Examples of women would be pointed out to me, and I'd be asked why I couldn't match them.

There was the mother who provided a home-cooked meal every night, despite running a home-based business. There was the mother-of-four/teacher/musician, paying a mortgage on her own. I have a friend, who has an admin job that she does from home. She had one child, and good family support. She earned enough money to pay for a gardener. She said that all mothers could do it all — after all, she could.

But they can't. Why else are women and children hit disproportionately by poverty, and end up in the food-bank queues? Why – when I went into the homes of other working single mothers, was I often met with a bomb-site of unwashed clothes and a sink of washing up? And an unkempt garden? Why couldn't I manage it all? I felt like a failure.

To the outside world, the suggestion was for me to work harder. If/when I was struggling financially, family and friends asked why I didn't do more plumbing — not considering that the job is physically exhausting, and that I was already exhausted from household chores and childcare.

Earn more. Work harder. I felt like a rat on a wheel, running hard but the wheel was slippery. I couldn't keep upright. My arms were flailing. I took the super-mum calendar, and — when I got home — I binned it. I couldn't bear to look at it. It upset me too much.

In the male world of work, the job comes first. I told my colleague about my latest run-in with our boss. As predicted, I'd been caught. But he just shrugged his shoulders.

"The job comes first," he said.

Which reminded me of the time, a few months earlier, when I'd been finishing a job with him.

Most times, we left work on time — and I could do the creche pick-up on time. But one day, our home-time came and went. We were about 20 minutes over. We were working in Bridport, about 40 minutes drive from the creche. Things would be tight for me. The creche staff would be waiting to go home, and I'd also be fined. Being late wasn't an option for me.

"I need to go," I said to him. "I have to pick up my children."

"No, you can't go," he said. "No one leaves until the work is finished."

"But it's past hours."

"That's just the way it is. You can't be a clock-watcher in this job."

My face must have been a picture of pain. He relented, and I bolted out to my car, and sped back to Weymouth. I got to the creche with only a couple of minutes to spare. I was so stressed that my hands were shaking as I released my grip on the steering wheel, and dashed into the building.

Time. TIME. Time. Everyone wanted more of my time. There wasn't enough of it. There wasn't enough of me to go round. And it was affecting my plumbing job. I didn't know how I was going to sort this out.

My mother tells me that employment prospects for women have improved during her lifetime. When I was a small child, it wasn't easy to even find childcare. I remember a succession of babysitters, who would eventually quit when they couldn't cope with the liveliness and sometimes naughtiness of me and my siblings. Partly because of better access to childcare, more women are now in the workforce.

I looked up some statistics. Fifty years ago, a little over a third of women aged 25 to 54 were in the labour force. In 2017 in the UK, around 80% of that age group did paid work. Also in 2017, 70% of mothers with partners, and 58% of lone mothers, had paid jobs. *19

And it's only fair that women can access jobs, pursue careers and have the same financial opportunities as men. The ability to earn one's own money brings choices about how we live our lives. And similarly, it's right that governments should push to retain the skills of talented women who become mothers.

When my first child was born, in 2008, I took maternity leave for nearly a year and then returned to my job part-time. That worked well. I negotiated an office-based, 9am-5pm role, which would fit in with creche hours. I'd be laying out pages and checking story content — something I could come and go from, according to days off and childcare.

After our second daughter was born, 16 months later, we returned to the UK. We were shocked at how competitive the job market was. We'd both had good jobs in Australia but couldn't find the same opportunities and wages in the UK.

Ken threw himself into job applications for ambitious career jobs that he would have been brilliant at. But despite getting onto the short list of many recruiters, the best jobs evaded him. There always seemed to be another candidate who had the edge on him.

And so he eventually settled for a lower-grade job on the newspaper in Weymouth. That's how we ended up living here. While he went to work, I stayed at home looking after our children. The local wages would barely have covered my childcare costs. I thought about looking for freelance writing and photography work, but I was so busy with the kids that I didn't get far.

But during this time, the comments of family members and people around me came as a shock. Those without children, or with grown-up children, didn't see the work that went into being a stay-at-home mum. One comment was "Oh wow, my friend has three children and she didn't take anywhere near as much time off as Jennie." Time off?

Another observed my daily trips to playgrounds and swimming pools with the kids.

"You have a nice life, don't you?" was her comment. It was a nice life — I loved being a mum. But her comment was tinged with judgement, as if all I did was drink tea and chat with other mums all day.

Another suggested that I take a night-time shelf-stacking job at the supermarket. I was staying with my parents at the time (while we set up our new lives in the UK.) My parents could watch the sleeping babies when I was on night shift. And then I'd be free to look after them during the day.

"When do I get to sleep?" I asked. "Despite the best intentions, I doubt I could last long on two hours a night."

When Ken was finally offered the Weymouth job, the four of us found a house to rent, and all moved here. And we settled into our new lives. Each morning, Ken went off to work. But when he came home, like many stay-at-home parents, I had nothing to show for my efforts.

I could have cleaned the kitchen floor several times, and a fresh layer of biscuit crumbs would have landed. Toys were continuously pulled out of toy boxes and flung across the room. And there were always snacks and meals to make, and nightly baths to supervise. All done typically with my youngest daughter strapped to my back in a baby carrier, as for months she insisted to either be continually cuddled or carried by me.

Let's say I'd been a nanny, and I was being paid for looking after the kids. Would I still have been referred to as having "time off" or having "a nice life?" I doubt it. With money changing hands, it would have been seen as 'real work'.

Ken was often frustrated at me, asking why I didn't 'do more", as in cook better meals, iron his shirts and do all the tasks that his friend's wives were supposedly doing.

"You're a housewife," he said. "It's your job to do these things."

How could I explain to him my daily grind when I didn't even know what I did myself? The hours just vanished into a blur of playgroups, swim lessons, meals and cleaning.

Though things were to get harder. When our marriage broke down, I became a single mum. I stayed in Weymouth, and found another house to rent. But I struggled financially, and my domestic workload was even higher. I had two children to feed/clothe/look after, a house to clean, a garden to control, bills to oversee, a car to maintain… the list went on. Typically of young children, they were often up in the night and I was sleep-deprived the next day.

I also attended college one day a week, in my initial plumbing training. I didn't yet have a work placement or job to go with it. So at the time, I wasn't meeting the onsite requirements. But just studying the theory, and being in the college workshop was of huge value to me. Going to plumbing college was one of the highlights of my week. I stepped out of my 'normal' life, and tapped into the old me. It made me feel alive. I loved being there.

I knew I'd soon be back in the world of paid work, hopefully as a plumber. But the job and its requirements were yet to be revealed. And — as I later discovered — working hours is a major factor.

Britons are working more and more hours each week. According to the trade union body TUC, the average working week in the UK, in 2017, was 43.6 hours a week. And almost four million employees in 2017 were working more than 48 hours a week, despite a European working time directive which aimed to limit those hours. *20

Since then, I've seen plumbing jobs advertised for 43 hours per week. I've seen lots of trade job adverts that carry overtime, and others that carry overnight/weekend on-call duties. It seems the former 37.5hr work week is becoming obsolete.

The survey also found that managers and professional staff worked the longest hours, with one in 25 men clocking up at least 60 hours a week. The TUC statistics didn't mention women.

Maybe because they've already quit their jobs, or turned down promotions. Long working hours and a lack of flexibility hits women hard. Survey after survey has found this to be a major cause of talented and educated women leaving their jobs. *21

A Harvard Business School study found that 62 percent of its female graduates with more than one child were either not working, or working part-time just five years after graduating.

These kind of hours are a barrier to mothers. And they aren't great for men either — many of whom would also like to spend more time with their families.

I know of fathers who want to attend school parent meetings, or medical appointments with their children, and battle for time-out from their employers. Often, they're not even asking for the whole day off — maybe just a couple of hours for the particular meeting. But the bosses are unwilling to let them go.

I've heard of men who have had to pull a sickie to get time out for a family holiday, when their employers have repeatedly said no — that the summer is too popular a time for everyone to have a holiday, and they can have their time off in the quieter months (when their kids are in school).

I know of one father who, when his second child was born, feared redundancy from a particularly demanding employer. Jobs were being shed every few weeks at his workplace, and one of the factors was productivity. As a result, he worked late into the evenings and weekends to stay competitive against his colleagues. Even though he was entitled to two-weeks of paternity leave, he didn't dare take any time off for fear of being marked out for redundancy.

So while mothers should receive equal access to jobs and opportunities, fathers should also be able to take up parenting responsibilities. The law has tried to address this, but it's not working.

As I found with my struggle to get to work on time, equality is too often taken as 'one rule for all'. If mothers want to do these jobs, then openings are available for them. But often, they are based on a traditional male work model, which she can't always fit into. And that model often isn't great for the fathers either.

Going back to my predicament, I was sure that legislation covered my problem.

I thought back, to the staff training I had to undertake, when I first joined the company. I'd sat through numerous videos, presentations and online courses, which looked at health and safety, and various legal issues — such as equal opportunities, discrimination (such as homophobia, or sexism) and other work practices.

One slide had caught my attention. It looked like an issue I might face. It was on the topic of sex discrimination. It was about a mother who struggled to get to work on time, due to childcare issues.

"Is this sex discrimination?" asked the slide.

'Yes' was the answer. It indeed was. It was classed as a gender issue, because women often take on much higher childcare responsibilities than men. And if something affects one gender more than another, it can be classed as sex discrimination if support isn't given. In this case, some flexibility from the employer to enable her to pursue her job should be given. This was my problem, precisely.

And I did some research. The law seemed to have moved on, and now provided for a wider range of flexible working, for both men and women. All employees have the legal right to request changes to their hours of work. As long as you've been working for your employer for 26 weeks (yes, I had) you can ask to work part-time, flexi-time, term-time only, or shifts that fit in with your childcare.

The employer must consider your request. They can only refuse under one of several business considerations, such as difficulties to run the business and provide available cover when you weren't there.

So surely, in my case, there wouldn't be any issue. I only needed a bit of flexibility, to allow me to balance childcare with the further-away worksites. It wouldn't be of particular difficulty to my team-mate, who could cope without me for 20 minutes on those difficult mornings. I didn't expect to be paid for those 20 minutes. But without that flexibility, I couldn't do my job.

I had to phone the manager. I had to explain my predicament, and the clash with my boss. I expected him to remember the videos we'd all sat through, but he didn't.

"Your hours start at that time," he said. "You need to be at work at that time. Childcare is your responsibility, not ours. We can't have one rule for you, and one for the men."

So, that summed it up. The world of work is built on male terms — especially if you're working in a traditional male industry, such as plumbing. I'm female. I was also a mother. My colleagues and bosses weren't accustomed to female workplace needs. I was treated like one of the blokes, as that is how they viewed equality. And I didn't know how I would find a way through this.

Chapter 10

Getting hurt – the risks of the job

All I did was roll over in bed. Not exactly dangerous stuff. Or not that you'd imagine. But it was enough to aggravate the knee injury that had kept me off work for the last few weeks, following my run-in with the boss.

Rob felt me roll over, and heard my kneecap crack. Again. It was loud enough to wake him up. Meanwhile, I woke up a split second later from the pain. It felt like a hot poker had been pushed into my knee joint. But as suddenly as the pain came, it went again, and I tried to get back to sleep.

The injury had been caused at work, in an attic. It had happened the day after I'd phoned the manager about my lateness — an issue that became obsolete overnight. I now had bigger issues to deal with. Like a movie in my head, I re-played the day of the injury.

I'd been at the beginning of a five-week project to upgrade the central heating systems in a series of bungalows in Lyme Regis. The plan was to strip out the old hot water cylinders and electric storage heaters and install radiators and a gas boiler in each property.

As the plumber's mate, it was my job to run the pipes — which in this case, would span the attic, dropping down to the radiators in the rooms below. I was apprehensive about that task. Easter was approaching, and the weather was already quite hot – warm enough to sunbathe on the beach. By late morning, it was more than toasty up in the attics. By early afternoon, it was unbearable.

How hot can attics be? The answer is… extremely hot. Some attics can be as hot as 55c. And even those that are insulated and ventilated can reach 10c above outside temperatures. To compare, such is the sun's power, the interior of a car can reach 38c after being parked in direct sun for just one hour. And that has been enough to kill numerous pets and small children over the years.

But you can take my word for it — it was hot up there. I was especially hot, as I was wearing an asbestos suit over my work uniform. Myself and a colleague had discovered this was an ideal way to protect our skin from the itchy fibreglass insulation up there.

It was a Friday morning. The time had come to run the attic pipes. Sunshine beamed through the downstairs windows, like a giant heat lamp. Opening the loft hatch was like opening an oven door — hot air awaited me as I hoisted myself up. It reminded me of when I first arrived in Australia, when I stepped out of the air-conditioned plane and into the tropical heat.

But I persevered. I climbed into the attic and started my work. But as the minutes passed, I got hotter and hotter. I was cooking. I had to keep retreating from the loft to cool down. Sometimes I'd barely last five minutes before retreating — much to the worried face of my boss, who was loitering at the foot of my ladder. I wasn't getting much work done.

Surely — I wondered — an employer had a duty of care regarding the work environment. This was extreme temperature. There was no ventilation up there. No fan. No air conditioning. Could cooling equipment be brought in? Maybe. But this was the real world, where health and safety rules don't always percolate down to the building site. Budgets and time demands don't always accommodate such things. I wasn't brave enough to bring up the subject.

The previous summer, when I'd still been the new girl, I'd watched my colleagues push through the discomfort. It had been a show of bravado and machismo, as they stripped off their shirts and worked topless, handling the challenge.

I'd been spared for a while. But I couldn't cope with the same temperatures as my male colleagues. Not only could I not remove my shirt, which seemed to buy them a slight relief. But I also didn't share their resilience to the high temperatures. It was obvious that — despite my best intentions — I would not be able to handle such a harsh work environment.

Was that because I was female? Maybe. In general, women don't retain heat as well as men. Science has confirmed that we're the first to feel the cold in winter. And it would seem I was not as good at keeping cool as my colleagues were in hot weather. But I was under pressure to keep up with them. I'd chosen to be there, working alongside them. I was young, and I was fit; I wanted to be able to do this.

But high temperatures weren't the only challenge. Already discovered that week was the lack of boarding in the attic. When I'd first popped my head through the loft hatch, I'd been met with a blanket of thick, yellow insulation. I couldn't even see the joists. A couple of plywood boards had been issued to me. I could lay them across my workspace – moving them as needed. But I'd still have to walk across the joists, carrying the boards, my work lamp, tools, copper pipe and fittings with me.

I hadn't received any specific training on attic safety. But I'd worked in plenty of un-boarded attics before (during colder weather), so I felt pretty confident. On that Friday, I discovered I could get around quite easily and quickly by clambering through the central cross-beams (upside-down wooden Vs}, twisting my feet into whatever toeholds I could find at the bottom of the V. It was a bit uncomfortable for my feet, but seemed like a good solution.

At one point, I swung my foot past a beam, put my arms around it, and pulled myself round and past it. But in doing so, I bent my knee, twisted my leg, and transferred my weight onto it. I had yet to learn this is a big no-no for knees. How often must I have made this move while playing football, snowboarding, surfing, etc? Most of the time, I bounce back from such manouevres. But not this time.

I felt something stretch in my knee. It didn't hurt. No pain — not at that moment anyway. But there was a definite sensation of something stretching inside my inner right knee joint.

Five minutes later, I was back down the ladder again to cool off. And I got the first indication that I might have injured myself. I couldn't stand on my knee. I couldn't put any weight on it at all. I held the bottom of the ladder, wondering what to do.

But just as quickly as the pain hit, it went away. My knee felt fine again. I had work to did. So I climbed back into the attic to continue my work. And aside from the heat, I was fine for the rest of the afternoon. And I thought that was the end of the matter.

Working in this job, I was always aware of the risk of injury. It was the first thing I studied, when I started college. Chapter one of my college textbook covered PPE — personal protection equipment. I learned about steel toe-capped boots, gloves, goggles, ear defenders, helmets, high-visibility vests and more. I learned about safe working practices, such as keeping work areas tidy, and checking equipment before use.

My tutor would recount countless tales he'd either seen or heard about, of on-site accidents. Such as people getting blinded from shards of tile (no goggles). Or blood poisoning (himself) after cutting his hand on a fluxed pipe end.

I heard of another female plumber who had removed a toilet during a refurbishment without wearing safety gloves. She dropped the toilet, and a sharp edge of porcelain sliced through the skin between her thumb and first finger. The injury involved a trip to A&E and stitches.

My classmates and I would sit, mouths open in shock, as he shared these lessons. We were all scared of becoming a statistic.

Health and safety was usually also on my employer's radar. The company had its own health and safety officer, who delivered regular presentations on ladder safety, safe lifting, how to recognise asbestos and the like. But attic safety had been overlooked.

In hindsight, I now appreciate the dangers of attics. Not only was there the risk of falling between joists (and through the ceiling), and the issue of hot/cold temperatures. But climbing — as I was — over and around the beams could also cause injuries. And I was doing all this in a poorly lit environment (I only had a plug-in work lamp), fed by an extension lead through the loft hatch.

Because of these dangers, some companies forbid their staff from working in un-boarded roof spaces. Had this caught the attention of our health and safety officer, I am sure he would have made it a priority. Equipment may have been available — albeit at a price — that could have provided me with temporary walkways, lighting and air conditioning.

However, there was a disconnect between our team and the office staff (including the health and safety officer). I'd noticed that the teams working on the tools resented the intrusion of the office staff. They didn't want to be told what to do by pen-pushers. After all, they were the experts of their trades. So sometimes, we'd go to the presentations — which were mandatory — only to revert to our standard work practices the moment we got back onsite.

Ladder safety was of particular concern for a colleague and me. It's risky. We'd been instructed (in the presentation) on how to carry ladders, check them for safety, the angle to prop them up, what surface to put them on, and how to secure a ladder. I was particularly interested to learn that we weren't to lean our ladders against guttering. Instead, we were to use a ladder stand-off (a frame that holds the ladder a small distance from the wall, so you are clear of the guttering).

Myself and my colleagues routinely leaned our ladders against guttering. Back onsite, that same afternoon, I reminded my line manager of this. But he said that this was the real world, not a conference room. We didn't have any ladder stand-offs. How else would we prop the ladder? And up the ladder he shimmied, encouraging me to follow. I didn't feel safe. The risk of falling off, and being badly injured was too real.

This particular line manager was keen to develop my ladder-climbing confidence. Despite having been a keen rock climber in my youth, I wasn't happy about climbing high ladders without safety ropes or the like.

Initially, my colleague surveyed my climbing technique. I was so nervous that I hugged the ladder as I went up it, with my knees splayed frog-like across it.

"No, no, no," he cried. "Stick your bum out. Relax. And you didn't need to grip it so tightly."

One tactic was to ask me to pass him a tool, while he was on a roof. This would involve me climbing up to roof height. Another time, he managed to coax me onto the roof. We had a series of shorter ladders — one up onto a garage flat roof, and another up the first floor, which met the roof ladder (hooked over the apex of the property).

I got up all this OK. Because they were shorter ladders, I managed to talk myself into thinking they were shorter heights. But I almost had a nasty accident on the way down. The roof ladder should have been secured to the wall ladder, which it wasn't.

At the time, I was still very early on in my training, and didn't know any better. As I clambered down from the roof ladder and onto the wall ladder, it wobbled under my weight. For a moment, I thought it was going to topple sideways — chucking me the height distance of a house to the ground below. But luckily, it stabilised. And I got down in one piece.

I told my boss about it later. He shook his head, and shivered. "I don't want to hear about things like that, Jennie," he said.

After the wobbly ladder incident, I refused to pass my first-floor windowsill threshold. And even today, I won't climb above that height. I'll pay someone else to come onto my jobs, and climb the ladder.

But this new reluctance annoyed my foreman.

"When you took this job, in your interview, you said you were happy to work at heights," he said.

I corrected him: "I said I was happy towork at heights if I feel safe. I don't feel safe on those ladders."

My colleague, also a plumber's mate, was similarly concerned. He was happy to climb the high ladders. But what if he got injured?

"I need to know what would happen if I fell off and got so badly injured that I was unable to work?" he asked. "I've got a family to support."

Would it be 'tough luck' as in 'you were trained and officially told not to take such risks' or would he receive financial compensation? He never got a straight answer.

But we knew the score. This was the gap between the official line and the "just do it" line. But what if we were injured? And our health and livelihoods were on the line? We couldn't shake our concerns. The boss couldn't answer this. Nor could our general manager. And so that particular dispute rumbled on.

Although a solution was on the way. New ladder-climbing equipment called Tetra was on the way.

Two or three team members would be chosen for the kit, as they'd need to be fitted with harnesses.

The system would involve the ladder being secured to the building, and the plumber being tied to the ladder. So if the plumber was to fall, they would be caught by a safety rope.

But we didn't yet have this equipment. And so neither of us would climb the tall ladders.

And now I'd been hurt at work. Not on a ladder, but doing a task I'd never imagined was risky, in an attic. Possibly, with adequate temporary boards, my accident may have been avoided. Or perhaps my knee was a ticking time bomb, just waiting for a reason to ground me. Another person, with a healthier knee, might have been OK.

Yes, I'd had an 'accident in the workplace, that wasn't my fault' — as quip the radio adverts. But there was no point in chasing financial compensation. One look at my medical records, which detailed years of knee problems, would mess up any claim. Far better to focus on getting strong again. My knee was far from OK.

I woke up on Saturday morning in pain. Yet again, I could barely put any weight on it. How would I manage work on Monday morning? I had two days to fix it. I tried everything I could think of — ice packs, ibuprofen to reduce the inflammation, and lots of rest with my knee elevated. I even went for a paddle in the sea, hoping the cold water might have an effect. And on Sunday night I went to bed, prepared to call in sick the following day. I'd been in pain all weekend.

However, it appeared a miracle had happened overnight. On the Monday morning, my knee pain had vanished. It was as if nothing had happened. I couldn't understand it. But off to work I went.

Back up into the attic I went. The weather had cooled off slightly, and I completed a full but uneventful day of work. All was fine — until the very final moments of the day. As I kneeled down to vacuum the tenant's carpet (to clean the mess we'd made — not do their housework), a sharp twinge hit my knee. I tried to stand up. The pain hit again. I couldn't put any weight on my knee. I stood, on one leg, balancing myself against the kitchen table. I was stranded.

"Are you OK?" asked the customer.

I laughed nervously. No. I explained my pain. My colleague came in, so I told him as well.

"Just give it a couple of minutes. You'll be OK," he said.

But even a couple of minutes later, it was still agonising to put weight on it. But nevertheless, I somehow shuffled around the house, and put the vacuum cleaner and my tools to one side for the next day. And I was free to go home.

But I had a problem. Another problem. My car was parked about five minutes walk away, at the bottom of a hill. I could barely walk. What was I going to do? My choices were to: 1. Ask my colleague for help. But I didn't want to hold him up — he wanted to go home too. And I was too embarrassed to ask for help. Besides, what could he did, other than drive me to the nearest hospital? I was more than an hour's drive from home. I didn't have time to go to the hospital. I had my usual end-of-day dash to collect the kids from childcare. Option 2. Struggle down the path on my own, take the pain, get to my car and drive home.

I chose option 2. And I was on a mission. The first part of my trip featured a handrail along the path, so I leaned on it and hopped along. So far so good. But once I reached the end of the rail, I was on my own. With tears in my eyes, I struggled through the remainder of my journey, each step becoming more painful than the last.

Somehow I managed to get to my car. And again I cried, both from the pain and my predicament, before I started to drive home.

In retrospect, I wasn't in a fit state to drive back to Weymouth. My right knee was throbbing. I could still drive, but only just. Through the tears and gritted teeth, I made it back to Weymouth, and back to the childcare centre.

And then I faced my second challenge. I had to walk into the childcare centre to collect my children. I suppose I could have phoned the centre, explained the issue and asked them to bring the children out. But I didn't.

Why? Because I wanted to be able to cope. I wanted to be able to push through this. I didn't want the childcare staff to worry, to question whether I was physically able to drive home and look after two children. And I didn't want to be an inconvenience.

This was just a painful knee. Just a bit more pain, then I'd be home. I had five minutes to collect the girls, before they closed. Such was the tight pick-up window I often faced between work and home. So in I went. I braced myself, pushed through the pain, and did what I had to did. And then I drove home, and phoned the girls' dad.

"Could you come over?" I asked. "I've hurt myself. I think I might need to go to hospital."

As I lay on my bed waiting for him to arrive, the pain intensified. My knee now hurt all the time, rather than just when I put weight on it. I couldn't find a comfortable position. And neither could I get back downstairs to find some painkillers. So I just waited for him.

Twenty minutes later, he was with us. After feeding the children, he helped me into the car, and the four of us went to the local hospital.

"You need a wheelchair," he insisted, much to my embarrassment. I didn't want to be pushed round, in a wheelchair. But he was right. I needed one. So off he went, to get one.

I was in too much pain for the doctor to examine me properly. Though I still managed to laugh when our youngest daughter, then aged seven, asked the staff if they'd 'fixed' me. She asked with such a stern, serious voice, in such an authoritative manner. I was laughing and crying at once.

'No, not yet," was the reply.

It would appear that I'd made my injury much, much worse by walking and driving on it. Now I had to face the consequences. I was sent home with painkillers, crutches and a referral for an NHS physio in two weeks' time. In the meantime, I was to stay at home, and rest.

First of all came the call of shame to my manager. I was already in his bad books for having been late for work.

More bad news from me. I dialled his number.

"Jennie." Was it a statement? I guessed my number was saved on his phone.

"Um, I have something to tell you. I have a problem…"

I was sitting on my bed, legs in front of me, crutches next to me. It all seemed so surreal. Like a dream. But I explained what had happened. And that I had a doctor's appointment booked, to get the all-important sick note so I could be signed off work.

The doctor's appointment came and went. The doctor was sympathetic — he'd also suffered from knee issues. He considered the nature of my job, and signed me off for four weeks.

I phoned my manager again, who groaned. "Why so long?"

"No worries," I said. "If my knee is better, I'll come back in."

"But you can't come back early," he said. "A doctor has signed you off, as being medically unfit for work. You're not allowed back on site until that time is up."

Woo hoo. Four weeks off. I was initially delighted at the prospect of being at home with my feet up for four weeks. But I never imagined I'd still be signed off after four weeks. That it would take more than four months, and lots of physio, before I could return to work. And even more time, and more physio, before I'd feel strong again. The NHS consultant referred me for an MRI scan on my knee. It could be a cartilage issue. But she couldn't give me any treatment until she knew what the issue was.

A couple of weeks later, I slid into a giant banging machine in Dorchester hospital, and had my knee scanned. Then back to the physio. The issue wasn't cartilage. I had a bit of arthritis, but that wasn't the cause either. It was muscular. She felt around my knee.

"Where's your muscle? There should be a muscle here." She felt around my knee again.

"I've found it. But it is very weak. There's hardly anything there. You'll need physio to build the muscles up."

She gave me an exercise to get me started. I was to roll up a towel, or grab a cushion, and place it between my knees. I'd then squeeze tight, using the inner knee muscles to do the work.

"If you could build these muscles up, you should make a full recovery," she said.

That was the good news. The bad news — I could be waiting for at least 13 weeks to receive physio sessions on the NHS. "I'll have lost my job by then," I said.

The alternative was a quick-fix steroid injection into my knee. But it could cause longer-term damage to my joint, and it wasn't a permanent solution. She seemed to really know her stuff. For the first time in my life, I'd been given exercises to build up my inner knee.

Previous physio-therapists had focussed on my outer thighs, which — this lady told me — were in good shape.

But because of the muscle imbalance, the stronger outer knee muscles were pulling the knee cap out of alignment. There was already some arthritis in the joint. Treatment should also look at re-tracking the knee cap.

I had access to private health insurance through my workplace. It included physiotherapy. Could I see her privately for treatment? She looked away.

"I couldn't give you my private practice details. I'm here working for the NHS today. It would be unethical," she said. "But there's nothing to stop you looking me up on Google when you get home. You've got my name. You'll find me."

So I looked her up, and booked myself in for what would be around ten, 40-minute sessions. And the following week, we set about 'fixing' my knee. She told me my muscle weakness was very common, and typically found in young women. But it was also commonly misdiagnosed. I'd be her third, current, female patient with this issue. The other two were making fantastic progress. One of them had even taken up jogging again. I could also make good progress if I put the work in.

I was at a junction. I saw that I could either put the work in, and regain my knee fitness, and my plumbing career and life that depended on that fitness. Or, I'd likely end up hobbling on my knee for the rest of my life, maybe in and out of hospital on steroid injections, and I would never return to my plumbing work.

"You'll likely need to do knee exercises for the rest of your life," she added. "This won't go away. But it can be managed. I like to teach my clients to manage their problems, so they can be empowered, and not rely on endless physio for the rest of their lives."

That sounded good to me. So we cracked on. During that summer, I did between two and three hours of physio a day. I got into a routine of three 40-minute sessions, featuring knee exercises, general core strength, and abdominal exercises. Having good overall strength was vital.

She also gave me a TENS machine — a box that delivers electric pulses via two pads that were placed on the skin, at either end of the weak muscle. I was only to do a few minutes at a time. It would make my knee muscles contract and relax in time with the pulse.

"This will take you to a 4 out of 10 for muscle strength," she explained. "After that, you'll need to build strength through exercises."

After a week of using the machine, I could already see results. A muscle started to emerge. It looked a bit like a small cucumber, bulging under my skin. Then it grew further, and blended into my general fatness on my inner thigh, so I couldn't make it out any more.

She also taught me how to find my kneecap and monitor its tracking. My kneecaps moved diagonally across my knee. They should just move up/down, in line with one's leg, when the muscles are activated. This would also need to be addressed.

Quite quickly, I also started to walk again, without crutches. Though progress did fluctuate. I found that after a heavy exercise session, my muscles were tired. This was a dangerous time, when I was more susceptible to twisting my knee again, and ending up on crutches again.

I began to recover. I was so grateful for both finally finding a physiotherapist to treat me and having the health insurance to pay for her. I was skint. After only a few weeks, my income dropped to statutory sick pay — then about £70 pounds a week. I had two children to support. I was topped up with housing benefit, but it didn't give me much for extras.

I looked further into the health insurance. It also covered dental and eyesight. So I had my eyes tested. I'd suspected for a while that I might need glasses, which the optician confirmed. Under the policy, I received free testing and free glasses.

I'd also been suffering from toothache. So I visited a dentist and found I needed a root canal. Not all the treatment was available on the NHS. So hurrah for my health insurance. After all this treatment, I received a letter from the health insurer. It was a routine statement, showing how much I'd claimed on the policy and how much future claims I had left. The policy had its limits. And I was reaching them.

The letter began by saying how glad they were that I'd made such good use of the policy.

I laughed. And laughed, and laughed. I'd maxed out the policy. Thankfully I didn't need to make endless claims — my physio wouldn't be needed forever. I was making good progress. But I had a long way to go. In one of the early sessions, my physio wanted to see what I could do.

"Let's start with something easy," she said. "I want you to squat down, onto the floor, without holding onto anything. And then to stand up again."

"That's not easy," I said. I couldn't remember ever being able to do that. They used to try to get me to did it at PE in school, and I never could. I didn't realise it was something that supposedly fit, healthy people could do.

I tentatively had a go. And very quickly started to wobble. Gravity pulled me down, and I was starting to fall. She grabbed my hands, and pulled me up.

"Sorry, I didn't realise you couldn't do that," she said.

I hadn't realised I was supposed to be able to do that. I hadn't done it in years. Another issue I'd had for ages was walking down hills, and down steps — it takes a good amount of knee strength to carry one's weight in a controlled way. So I used hills and steps to mark my progress.

As the weeks went by, I was starting to get stronger. So Rob and I took ourselves off on a beach walk on Portland. It involved climbing down some steep steps to the beach.

My fledgling knee muscles started to kick in. I'd never felt muscles on the inside of my knee before, supporting me down the steps.

It didn't take long before they started to tire, and I was wobbling and unstable. But I'd seen what could be achieved, and what a healthier knee might be like. My physio was delighted, both with my progress and my pleasure.

"That's your new muscles starting to work," she said. "So, how about getting you back to work? It's not good to be off work — you'll get depressed."

"What me? No chance."

I didn't have time to be depressed. As in addition to looking after two children, and a huge amount of physio — which now included gym sessions and bike rides — I had a plumbing qualification to complete. I was at the end of a two-year advanced plumbing qualification, to NVQ3 standard, which would also give me Gas Safe certification. I was almost there.

But during those two years, I'd fallen behind in my studies. The entire class had. The college tutors couldn't even keep up with the lessons. Plans were afoot to over-run into September and October, to push us all through.

This worried me. I wanted to finish the qualifications.

I had time on my hands to study. So into my books I dived. Most of the core exams had been sat. But the gas safety exams remained, which was a huge study area. Plus I'd also need onsite assessments from my tutors. How would I figure those assessments out? I wasn't at work. And I had a very dodgy knee. It wasn't safe for me to be on a worksite.

That's even if I had a job to go back to. My employer had set me on a conveyor belt of time-based milestones that would cause me to lose my job if I didn't return within a certain period. It wasn't long – only about six months. And quite rightly, they were concerned about me going back early, and were concerned about the safety aspects of my injury. What would happen if my knee collapsed when I was atop a ladder? Well, as we all know — it wouldn't be a good outcome.

So this wasn't an easy challenge. The hardest aspect was the time limits put on me. A lack of time to finish the course, and to also re-build my knee. As hard as I was pushing, I needed more time. As is often the case. But I wouldn't let this beat me.

Chapter 11

Climbing the career ladder

While recovering from my knee injury, I had plenty of time off work to study.

I hit the textbooks in a big way, and spent two weeks solidly reading my gas books. I also found a way to complete the onsite logbook and assessments. I might not have been at work, but why should that stop me from going plumbing? Why should I be in paid employment to complete my gas engineer logbook?

My friends all had boilers, some of which needed fixing. And my tutor — who was a registered Gas Safe engineer and also an onsite assessor — could be both the mentor and assessor of the tasks.

And that is how I proceeded. I lined up a suitable array of boilers, and arranged to visit them with my tutor, and work through the tasks. Several mornings, I went to the college to drag him away from his desk, and drive him around the various houses. Which he dutifully did.

First we serviced a friend's combi boiler. All good. Then we fixed another friend's boiler — it had a leak, which had blown the fuse. She'd been without hot water or heating for over a year, choosing to spend her limited funds on vet bills rather than home maintenance. So she was delighted.

We also went to Rob's house, and serviced his back boiler. At the time, we'd only just started dating. He'd lived in the house for more than ten years, and had never had it serviced. Having done all this, the college arranged for me —and some of my classmates — to finish our training at a specialist gas training centre just outside Bournemouth. This would be an intensive two weeks — the first week would be spent training, and the second week on exams and assessments.

Anyone who doubts the intelligence of gas engineers should think again. They're among the most creative, problem-solving, hard-working and down-to-earth people I've ever met.

These were the hardest exams I'd sat in my life. I'd previously sailed through my A levels, an undergraduate degree, and a postgraduate degree. I'd been a brilliant student. But none of this had been as demanding as my time at the gas training centre.

The biggest challenge was taking on so much information in such a short amount of time. My classmates and I should have arrived knowing much more than we did, having been taught more about the basics of gas and gas appliances at our local college.

Our tutors in Weymouth knew their stuff. They were all experienced plumbers and boiler engineers. One of them still went plumbing at weekends, as he found it relaxing. But at college, they were always run off their feet. Only 15 of us were in the class, but there was a mountain of paperwork and logbooks to get through. We were only in college for one day a week, and the tutors couldn't keep up with the course and its requirements.

Some afternoons we were sent home while they caught up on paperwork. At the time, I was grateful for the time out. We all were. Many of us had families, and it gave us a brief chance to catch up on chores. Or sleep. Both are very valuable. But over the two years, we'd fallen behind with the course requirements. And on arriving at the gas training centre, the gaps in our knowledge were frowned upon.

There were two tutors at the training centre, whom we

dubbed 'good cop' and 'bad cop.' The nice guy explained things to us. His partner snapped at us, for not knowing things. This was one of my conversations with the 'bad' cop.

"Jennie, can you tell me what this part is?"'

I looked it up and down. It was a little box, with a wire coming out of it. We were standing by a gas cooker, so obviously something off the cooker. Some kind of electrode? Or flame supervision device? He wanted the precise terminology.

"Um, electrode?"

"No."

"FSD?"

"No. Why do I get the impression that you don't know, Jennie?"

"I do know. I know what it does. I just can't think of the name."

"I'm not convinced."

The first week of training flew by. We then had a week of exams, with a series of written papers that just kept coming. Followed by practical exams. Everyone felt the stress. But we all got through and emerged as newly qualified Gas Safe engineers.

I went home, and celebrated by taking the children out to dinner. The youngest didn't even know what we were celebrating — such reasons weren't relevant to her. More important was where we were going. They insisted on going to a pub with a play centre. So I took a book, and I ate and read while they bounced around.

The next day, I took my youngest daughter to a football match, where her dad joined us. To my embarrassment, I burst into tears on the sidelines. The trigger was something very trivial. But I was so frazzled by the gas training, that something had to give.

"You'd cry too, if you'd just gone through gas exams," I said. He looked dubious. He also was a university graduate. What could be so hard about gas exams? If only he knew. But I'd passed.

That chapter of my life was behind me. New challenges awaited. So out with the old challenges, in with the new. Life is full of challenges. As soon as one is solved, another will fill the void. I needed to pull my head out of my books, and reassess where I was at.

My knee was much better. Not perfect, but it was more stable and reliable than it had been. And I'd passed my gas exams. But new challenges were on the horizon. In particular, I was about to start a new plumbing job.

During the summer, I'd seen a Facebook advert for a job opening with a local plumbing firm. They wanted another gas engineer. So I applied. In my imagined best-case outcome, I hoped to introduce myself and be kept in mind for future posts when I had picked up more experience.

When I applied for the job, I still hadn't qualified. But to my surprise, I was offered the job. They were so keen to have me that they were happy to wait a few weeks for me to get through my gas exams. And they weren't worried about my knee.

"People get injured, and people get better," they said in the interview. "You're doing the physio. We don't see it will be a problem."

The position would be a step up from my previous job at the housing company. I'd have more responsibility and take steps to become a more experienced engineer. So I took the job, albeit with some anxiety.

"You'll be fine," said my friends and family.

But how could they be so sure? They're nice words of encouragement, but empty. No one knows how something will pan out. All one can do is prepare one's best, and face the outcome.

My new job was with a family firm, that had been around for more than fifty years, and had a great reputation in the community.

'We have a very low staff turnover,' I'd been told at my

interview. 'Our staff tend to stay with us for years. There's only one guy we had to let go, because he was turning up to work drunk."

So I turned up for work, at 8am on my first day, full of enthusiasm and optimism. I walked through the doors, wondering if this would be my workplace for the next 30 years. Little did I guess that I'd barely last ten weeks, two of which would be the Christmas shut-down.

I never imagined that I'd go home for lunch on the second day, and phone Rob in tears because I couldn't cope with the tasks. Nor that I'd be allocated the 'apprentice from hell' — an ambitious but arrogant young man, who refused to follow my instructions, which caused so many onsite problems. I wasn't fine. Far from it.

On that first morning, there had been paperwork to complete — a fat health and safety ringbinder file to read. I flicked through it. A lot of it looked important, such as procedures for lone working, and being the last one to sign off at night.

As I leafed through it, various managers — all brothers, fathers or uncles to each other — wandered in, to meet me. They seemed like nice guys.

"I wouldn't worry too much about reading all that," said one of them. "Just sign the form, saying you've read it. Then you can go out on your jobs. We've got a whole day of work lined up for you."

So I speed-read what I could. And then grabbed the job details and addresses, and off I went.

Already, I was lacking experience. I'd not done a lot of general repairs — such as leaking stoptaps, toilets, or pipes. I was fresh out of college. I was slow at such things. And unsure of what my boss expected of me. What parts should I carry on the van? Did I have adequate tools? I didn't feel prepared.

Years later, such jobs would be second nature to me. Challenging? Yes, sometimes. But I'd be able to handle most things that came my way. But back then, I was still learning. By mid-afternoon, I'd still only got through three jobs, out of six. My other jobs were reallocated to my various colleagues — whom I had yet to meet.

And so Day Two arrived. I met the lad who'd be my apprentice. He'd been at college the previous day. In his early 20s, I saw that he was strong, intelligent, keen to learn, but also very arrogant.

"The gas exams are a piece of piss," he declared. "They're not worth the paper they're printed on. An idiot could pass those exams."

Right. That hadn't been the experience of myself and my classmates the previous week. But never mind. He'd find out in time.

We set off to our first job together — a boiler swap-over in a town centre flat. I'd been given a small white ten-year-old Volkswagon Caddy van. My toolbox slid around in the back as we left the yard. Did I have enough tools? The right tools? I had no idea. But off we went.

We found the flat, where the most senior member of the company met us. Despite being in his 80s, he still took a hands-on role in the company. He gestured to the wall.

"New boiler goes back up here. You'll need a condense pump. The electrician will be along later to wire it up. Alright?"

He frowned. I didn't know what to say. His gruff manner didn't invite questions — or even doubts. Under Gas Safe rules at the time, I should have been working under supervision from a more senior engineer for a six-month probation period. My gas card hadn't even come through. But off went the old man, leaving me to take charge of this boiler install.

Immediately, I was out of my depth. For a start, we were in a first-floor flat above a busy street. How were we to drain down? What about ladder access to the flue? What about a ladder — I didn't have one. I only had hand tools. And how to install a condense pump? I'd never seen one before, let alone installed one.

At lunchtime, I phoned Rob in tears. I described the job to him. I didn't know what I was doing, let alone task a new apprentice on the job. I'd never removed an old boiler before. I'd never done a combi swap over — I'd only worked on new installs.

I didn't know how to drain the system — I couldn't find a drain valve, and was unsure where to run the hose pipe. And how to safely replace the flue? Shouldn't we be taking precautions to protect passers-by and traffic, as well as to protect ourselves? As the plumber onsite, all this was my responsibility. And that kind of responsibility should never have been put on me so soon.

In my interview, over the summer, I'd been assured I wouldn't be "thrown in at the deep end." That I'd be supported into the role. I'd also been assured that — aside from basic hand tools — all equipment would be supplied. But I was in the deep end, with barely any tools. And even less experience.

You couldn't be much less experienced. I'd only qualified as a gas engineer the Friday before. My gas engineer registration hadn't even yet been processed. I'd told my new bosses about the six-month probation period that morning, and my lack of a gas card, but I'd been told not to worry about it. They would take care of such matters. And then I'd been put in charge of a job, with a responsibility I hadn't expected so soon.

The morning had been a disaster. We'd started by turning off the boiler and draining down. But we couldn't find a drain valve. Sometime mid-morning, the apprentice's friend — another junior at the company — popped by. He found a drain valve under under the kitchen units. So we could at least drain the system.

But more problems. We didn't know where to run the hose. We were in an upstairs flat, on a busy street. Our hose pipe wasn't long enough to reach the drain a little distance down the street. So we emptied the water into the road.

Unfortunately, we didn't shut the drain valve afterwards. Excess water dripped through, down through the ceiling to the shop below. And an angry shopkeeper demanded money for damaged toilet roll in his store room. Ten pounds should cover it, he thought. So I fished £10 from my wallet, and paid him off. I wouldn't be claiming this back from my new bosses. I'd rather they didn't get to hear about it. And I shut the drain valve.

And then I was stumped. The office said they had a ladder we could use, if we picked it up. How would I fit it in the van? It didn't have a roof rack? And there was heavy traffic in the street below — where was I to foot the ladder? And who would climb it? And how to remove the flue? I'd never removed an old flue before.

Looking back on this, as I'm writing, I now have the experience to handle this job. It should have been planned a lot better — way before I arrived onsite to begin the work. A lack of planning would be typical at my new workplace.

"What are they thinking?" said Rob, as I described the morning to him. He was incredulous. "You shouldn't be in this position."

"I don't know what to do," I sobbed.

"You have to phone your boss," he said. "They shouldn't have done this to you. You need help."

So that's what I did. I'd been phoning my boss all morning. So I phoned again, after lunch, and updated him on the problems I was having.

Late afternoon, help arrived. And I met my another three of my new colleagues. They'd been pulled off their own jobs to help. One lad arrived with a ladder, which he shimmied up and then removed the flue. And two engineers — one in his 20s, the other in his 50s, attended to the boiler.

I stood aside, and watched them do what should have been my job. By the end of the day, the boiler was on the wall, wired up, plumbed in, and working. I was left to commission it (something I could do). I discussed my lack of experience with my new colleagues, and wondered why the bosses had put me in such a position.

"Oh, they are naughty," said one of them. "They do this all the time. They promise things at the interview, and then just drop you in it. They shouldn't have done this to you. It's not your fault. You're not ready to do this yet."

And I wasn't. I'd studied hard, and had qualified. Yes, there had been onsite assessments and logbooks to compile. There had been a lot of practical, onsite work. But I still had so much to learn. That's why the six-month probation period was in place — to put the new knowledge into practice with guidance and supervision.

At the time, the Gas Safe qualifications were due to be redesigned. They were to become harder, with a more vigorous practical element. And with good reason. It's a practical job, which demands a high level of skill and safety awareness.

I don't think you can be over-prepared to go onsite. All knowledge is valuable. All these years later, I still sometimes feel like a newbie. The more I learn, the more I realise I don't know. There are just so many different boilers and installations out there, spanning decades. I've got a handle on the basics, and more. But there's so much to master. I'll always be learning, and facing new challenges. But back then, to master so much at once was too ambitious.

With the help of my new colleagues, I got through the second day. And more support was given to me, on my following boiler installs. But in those early days, I was so overwhelmed and stressed that I wasn't performing well. I just couldn't think straight. Even simple stuff felt hard. I was on red alert, continually. Two weeks into my new job, my new bosses had a re-think.

"You're not as experienced as we expected," they said.

Why they thought I'd be more experienced, I didn't know. My words at my interview had been, "Obviously,

I'm lacking experience..." It takes years to become an experienced plumber.

I still hadn't been given a contract to sign. It eventually materialised, with lower hourly pay than had been agreed. I'd also be on a zero-hours contract, with no obligation of them to provide me with work or pay.

The lower pay was to be applied retrospectively. This didn't seem right to me, as I'd already worked the hours. And I'd given up a previous job partly for the higher wages. But what could I do? I wasn't in a position to bargain with them. So I signed the contract.

And so the weeks rolled by. Sometimes I'd be helping out on other installs. Sometimes I'd be running my own install. I became part of a team with my colleagues. We would jump in and out of other's jobs, as needed. Often, we were fighting against the clock. I discovered other team members were skipping lunch, so they could finish the jobs.

"But our managers tell us to take our lunch," I said.

"Oh, Jennie," they sighed. "They don't mean what they say."

Corners were cut on jobs. I noticed bottles of central heating cleaner chemicals stacked up in our warehouse.

Before new boilers were installed, the chemicals should have been used to flush the radiators and central heating systems.

Officially, we were told to do the flushing. But this would have added at least two hours onto the jobs, for just a very basic cleanse. This was time we didn't have. Boxes were ticked on commissioning forms saying the systems had been cleaned. Yet there were all these bottles in the warehouse. It wasn't being done.

More problems presented themselves. One minor issue was my work van. A warning light was permanently on the dashboard.

"Don't worry about that," said the brothers, who reckoned it was insignificant.

For a few weeks, the van was OK. But then, problems arose. A couple of times, it started to lose power as I was driving along. And then, one day it lost power completely. I glided to a stop on the grass verge. As luck would have it, a police car was coming the other way. The driver stopped, got out and came over.

"What's wrong?" he asked.

I explained. He thought for a moment, and then came up with the reason. The warning light was showing a red coil.

"It's a diesel engine," he said. "That's to do with the pre-heat for the engine. If you give it a few minutes to cool down, you should be able to drive again."

He was right. And I was soon on my way. But barely ten minutes later, I'd glided to a stop again. On another main road. Again, I waited, and got going again. When I finally made it back to my workyard, the van was taken away for repairs. And that was my next major lesson: Don't Ignore Warning Lights on Vehicle Dashboards.

More challenges, and more issues were to follow. Another, more serious issue, was a lack of communication between the office staff and the engineers. The managers would sometimes come onsite and do things but not update me — the plumber running the job — on exactly what they had done. Sometimes they'd come and go without my even realising.

On one job, I discovered an old asbestos water tank in the property. The managers came out to remove it. A hosepipe was run, and the system was drained.

Or at least I'd thought it had been drained. When I went to cut out the pipework to the cylinder below the tank, I discovered that they hadn't drained the cylinder. Water was flooding from the open pipe end that I'd just cut. I ended up sitting there, my thumb over the pipe, until my apprentice returned onsite and could pass me a fitting to cap the pipe.

That was another important lesson to me. Don't Make

Assumptions. In retrospect, I could have given the cylinder a nudge to see if it felt heavy. But I hadn't checked. In future, I would check everything.

Another major issue was my apprentice. We didn't get along. There were several reasons for this. The main issue was that he refused to take instructions from me. Unless one of the managers was around, he'd ignore me. He refused to acknowledge my — albeit limited — increased knowledge and experience. He didn't see why he should do the menial tasks on the install. Nor why I should be in charge.

This led to several incidents. Generally, they were trivial. Such as ringing up another apprentice to ask questions, rather than ask me — even for something as simple as how to bleed a radiator. He'd also ring up the office, without my knowing, and try to organise our jobs. And the managers would let him.

We were also very different people. We didn't see eye to eye. For a start, he drove too fast for my liking. He'd tailgate vehicles in front of us. And we had different values. He'd wash and style his hair before work in the mornings —something I never did, even when I'd worked in an office.

I found him materialistic, lacking empathy, no sense of humour and generally unlikeable. He didn't like me much either. I suppose taking the piss out of him in my first week didn't help. Back in my previous job, I'd been the queen of banter. It had been a sport. Everyone entered into it, with enthusiasm and good-humour. We teased each other relentlessly. And had a lot of fun doing it.

But I misjudged the banter in my new job. Despite going in gently, I got it wrong.

On one such occasion, there were four of us — two engineers, and two apprentices — in a kitchen. It was the end of the day. We'd joined forces to finish a job. We were watching my apprentice, atop a step ladder, fixing up a boiler flue. He was chatting away, telling us how skint he was as an apprentice, and how he had taken an evening job delivering pizza as he needed the money.

I made some stupid remark about "yes, so he can afford to eat." It was a weak banter. Not to my usual witty standard. But it took my new colleagues by surprise, and they burst out laughing.

My apprentice said I was a moron. We'd barely been working together for a week. Our working relationship went downhill quickly after that. We couldn't work together. We were notorious. Our colleagues would ask us "not to fight" when they left us together. So the bosses had another re-think.

"We're going to split you up," they said. "We're going to look after you, Jennie. We're going to train you to be a gas repair engineer."

I was delighted. This was a great opportunity. They planned to put me under the supervision of one of their more senior engineers, who would teach me about servicing and repairing gas appliances. So off I went.

And I loved my new role, and the time I spent with that engineer. His name was Mark. A heavy smoker, and bit rough around the edges — some of the customers were uneasy around him. But he was a top guy. Down-to-earth, fair, honest, reliable. And he was a great engineer. I loved going out plumbing with him.

And so more weeks rolled by. Christmas was upon us, and a 10-day shutdown. A little newsletter was produced by the management, thanking us all for our hard work. And also declaring how much progress I'd made in my new job. All seemed well.

Though not everything was well. I still had problems. My hours were 8am to 5pm, with 40 minutes for lunch. Five days a week. These were similar hours to my previous job, and with less travelling. I expected it all to feel easier, now I didn't have so drive to far to and from work.

Yet the opposite happened. I was exhausted. This new job was so much faster-paced and intense. And in conjunction with my busy home life, I'd never been so tired in my life. It wasn't sustainable.

I toyed with asking my bosses if I could drop down to a four-day week. But on returning after Christmas, I held back on asking. Something didn't feel right. I carried on going out on servicing jobs with Mark. And also doing the odd boiler install with the team. Yet I sensed my days were numbered. And I was right.

A couple of weeks into January 2016, on a Friday afternoon, I was asked to report to the office at 4pm. Just before home time. My colleagues were anxious.

"We don't feel good about this," they said.

And my former apprentice was also worried. We were a close-knit team. We might not always have got on, but we banded together to support each other through our daily jobs. They were good guys.

"You're all being paranoid," I said. "There are so many reasons why they might need me to pop by."

So off I trotted. I sat on the sofa in my boss's office, and waited to hear what he had to say. He came straight out with it.

"We're letting you go," he said. "It's not working out for us."

And that was that. No explanation. Apparently, their 'HR department' wouldn't let him give a reason. What HR dept? There was only the brothers, plus an admin assistant. I'd be given one week notice. He shrugged. He had nothing else to say. But I was furious.

"You said I was doing well, on that Christmas staff report," I said. "I gave up a job to come here. Now I don't have a job. What has changed?"

He wouldn't look me in the eye. I grabbed my bag, my coat, and stomped out. And I drove straight to Rob's house, and into his arms.

"I've lost my job," I said. "And I didn't do anything wrong."

But something had changed. That week, a big Dorset

plumbing firm went bust. Numerous experienced gas engineers were suddenly available, looking for work. Possibly for lower wages, in their hurry to find work. We figured that might have had something to do with it.

I wasn't going to work out my notice. How on earth was I expected to turn up, get stuck into my work, knowing I'd been sacked? So on the Monday morning, I phoned in sick. A couple of days later, I popped in to return their van, and to retrieve my tools.

And that was it. I was unemployed. I returned to sign on at the Job Centre while contemplating my next move.

Chapter 12

Not just one of the girls

Imagine that you had green skin, and that you were a minority, as most of the people around you had blue skin. In fact, for one of you there were 99 of them. You were massively outnumbered. The blue-skinned people doubted your worth. Some of them were nice to you, and encouraged you to join them. As long as you didn't outshine them. But in general, you were met with scepticism, a lack of support and understanding, and occasionally hostility.

But there were other green-skinned people like you, and they formed a little club that supported and encouraged each other. The blue people said it wasn't fair to have an exclusive club. But you needed that club, to help you participate in wider society. This is what it is like being a female plumber. And this is why, in 2016, I joined a women's plumbing group called Stopcocks.

Stopcocks was — and still is — a small organisation that supported women in the plumbing industry. A key part of their program was mentoring and telephone support. Plumbers could live anywhere in the country, and always have access to a friendly voice and technical support on the end of a phone.

At the helm were two women: an experienced plumber, Hattie, and her life/business partner, Mica.

I'd known about Stopcocks for years, having come

across them when considering what career to retrain into. I'd even gone to one of their regular picnics in a London park, wanting to find out more. And what a discovery.

I'd been in awe of them all. Their plumbers seemed so confident. And so knowledgable. And strong. And bubbly. I'd wanted to be one of them.

"I don't know everything," one of them said to me. "I know a lot. But we all need some help sometimes. You can train and earn money at the same time," she said. "Just stick to the easier jobs, and get paid for it.

"You can work when you want — some girls already have full-time jobs, and go plumbing at weekends until they're ready to do it full-time. And you can earn good money doing it."

It sounded great. But at the time, I was a full-time mum to two toddlers. I'd know when the time was right to join them. But in the meantime, I knew they were there and what they were about.

So when my second employer sacked me, they instantly came to mind. I'd always intended to join them one day. The time had come. I ran through my reasons:

1. I didn't want another employer. I didn't want to be scared of being sacked again. Everyone I knew, working for a salary, seemed scared of this.

2. I wanted to be my own boss, and to run jobs as I saw best. I didn't want to be pressured to fit into a boss's over-ambitious idea of time. For a start, I'd give myself time to flush heating systems on boiler installs. I wouldn't cut corners.

3. I could set my own days and hours, and work schedule, to suit myself and my family. In theory, at least. It would always involve some juggling, but a major consideration would be setting a realistic work/life balance.

And there was also another reason I joined Stopcocks. It was the 'herd' mentality. I wanted to be in a group of people like me — i.e., female. I wanted to be with people who celebrated femininity and were also strong, confident and brilliant plumbers. I needed them as role models, to show me that I wasn't misguided or wrongly ambitious in my new career. And I also needed to be with people whom I could work alongside without gender politics coming into play.

I could have all this with Stopcocks. There was no way I wanted to embark on self-employment on my own. Not when I was fresh out of college with so little experience. I'd depend on Stopcocks' support and guidance.

It was their phone support I was especially after. I needed the security of knowing there'd always be someone to ring if I had a question. Although I already had local plumbing friends I could contact, I didn't want to overwhelm them with constant phone calls.

Stopcocks would also take phone calls from prospective customers. I didn't have to worry about missing phone calls or jobs. Mica would take the calls, and log their details on a database, and I'd receive a text message to give them a call.

By that time, Stopcocks had already been running for numerous years. When I joined, there were six other plumbers on their books. I was a bit surprised there weren't more. But no matter — I figured, they'd have more time to give me attention, when I needed it.

So I got back in touch with them. Contracts were signed. I paid a joining fee of £450. A work uniform including a branded jumper, coat and t-shirts was sent to me. And a start date of May 13, 2016 was set.

It was slightly sooner than I was ready for. I had so much preparation to do. Top of my list was to buy a van. I didn't want anything too big — I needed to drive it onto customers' driveways, and park on narrow streets, and so on. Ideally, it would be a three-seater, so I could use it to drive the girls around. But very few small vans came with three seats. So I resigned myself to financing both a car and a work van.

It didn't take long to find a van. A painter/decorator in a nearby village was selling a 12-year-old Citreon Berlingo. It had a full service history. An MOT. A roof rack. Perfect. £750 later, and it was mine. I drove it home, and started kitting it out for my new business.

There was no racking inside. So I built various cubbyholes and shelving for my tools, ladders, bags, towels, dust sheets and other supplies. I also bought a pipe carrier — a long, metal tube — to go on the roof rack. It was grey. So I bought some cans of paint, and sprayed it bright pink. I sprayed the rest of the roof rack as well. And I bought some hot pink seat covers. And I fitted some curtains to the back windows, to hide the expensive tools I was carrying. It looked awesome.

More tools were needed. I invested in a flue analyser (it measures various gases in a boiler flue), as well as a wet vac, a multi-tool and blades, an extendable ladder, and more hand tools. And I loaded them into the van. My set-up costs, including the van, Stopcocks fees and some advertising, came to just under £3,000. It cleared out all my savings. But it seemed like a good investment.

Finally, I named the van. Betty. As in Betty The Berlingo. And I was ready to hit the road. And so began a four-year stint with Stopcocks, and the next chapter of my adventure.

I loved being in Stopcocks. They helped me set the business up — which mainly involved putting adverts in local newsletters, and getting the local newspaper to write a story about me. The jobs started to come in. So out I ventured. As promised, Hattie was always on the end of the phone to give technical advice. Some days, I'd be ringing her constantly during a job. Another day, I might not pick up the phone at all. But in the absence of a boss watching over me, I needed her there, ready to catch me.

My van became a visible presence on the streets of Weymouth. During my first trip out in it, I was stared at by other van drivers. It was quite a unique vehicle. Years later, they're all used to me. But at first glance, my van turned heads.

"I always know when you're in my street," Rob said. "I see a pink streak through the window, and know you'll be knocking on my door a couple of minutes later."

Initially, I was shy about going into the plumber's merchants. Part of me felt like I shouldn't be there, like I was trespassing into a male domain. But I needn't have worried. It wasn't an issue. Weymouth already had two other female self-employed plumbers. The merchants were used to women. I was just another face to serve.

Sometimes, if I venture out of Weymouth, and up the hill into Dorchester and the merchants there, I'm stared at by other customers. But it doesn't bother me anymore. I have bigger things to consider, such as my work. But back then, it took some courage to go into these merchants, especially in my new work outfit.

My Stopcocks uniform featured a black collared t-shirt with a small logo on the chest — the words 'Stopcocks Women Plumbers' and a swirly logo next to it. I had a jumper to match.

It was the jacket that grabbed the attention. Also black, on the back it had the words Stopcocks Women Plumbers in big white words. It was probably visible from space. One day, one of the sales staff leaned close and quietly said: "Jennie, those words are rude."

"What words? Oh, those? Stopcocks? Yeah, I suppose they are," I replied.

For a while, I didn't wear my jacket into the merchants. But as the weather got colder, I couldn't bring myself to shed it — the fleecy lining just felt too nice against my skin. So I started to wear it again. No one else commented on my jacket. Well, not in the merchants, anyway.

The name Stopcocks created a lot of amusement in the business networking group I'd joined. We'd typically introduce ourselves and our businesses each meeting, for the newcomers. Every time, my companions would burst out laughing upon hearing the name Stopcocks. They thought it was one of the best business names they'd heard, considering the nature of the organisation.

Despite being in a traditional male profession, I was mainly surrounded by women. Most of my customers were older women. Some of them had husbands, but their husbands were pushed to one side as their wives oversaw my visit.

Sometimes the husbands were involved, but it was on an equal footing with their wives. It was so unexpected to see these household dynamics. It hadn't been my experience in my parents or friends homes when I was growing up. But plumbing began to feel like a normal, natural thing for me to do.

Research shows that there's a lot of customer demand for tradeswomen, be it plumbers, electricians, painters, gardeners, or whatever. A significant number of homeowners feel more comfortable inviting a woman into their home (rather than her male equivalent). Their reasons: other than personal safety, they expect the woman to be more trustworthy, more respectful of their home, to pay more attention to detail and be easier to get along with.

Of course, that's just their perception. Being female isn't a guarantee. There are dishonest people of both genders out there. But having said that, I came across an article in The Daily Mail newspaper that found that some female and elderly customers were being charged up to 50% more than middle-aged men for simple plumbing repair jobs. *22. I understand why customers may be nervous of tradespeople.

But I have also seen that for a woman to succeed in this industry, she is more likely to be passionate and determined about her career choice than her male peers — who may have ended up in plumbing college having flunked their GCSEs. It takes a huge amount of effort for a woman to break into plumbing. She doesn't end up in the industry by accident.

Many female students end up being top of their class in their plumbing exams. I was, and so were other female plumbers I've met.

One woman I know studied so hard for her gas exams that the assessor said she was the best prepared, most knowledgeable student he'd met. And she thought she was rubbish, and was going to fail. That's typical of the women plumbers I know. They study hard, and work hard and sometimes still under-estimate themselves.

In my college class, my male colleagues were openly competitive. I used to pretend I wasn't bothered about my grades, and coming top of the class when our exam results were announced. But inside my head, I was skipping merrily around. I'm as competitive as anyone. A lot of women are. But we don't tend to show it. We're not encouraged to show it, especially when we're competing against men.

But we're not just bookworms. Customers report that tradeswomen are better at communicating, and don't tend to talk down to them. Some female customers feel that male plumbers ignore them and speak to the male in the room, or speak to the space next to them that their male partner might occupy.

I talk a lot to my customers. I want them to understand their plumbing systems and the work I'm doing for them. So I explain my work. And by talking about their plumbing issues, I can get the information I need more. And they feel more comfortable and confident in my abilities.

Some customers are very interested in me and my work. It's not by accident that they book a female plumber. One woman, in her 60s, desperately wanted to get her hands on my tools. She needed a new float valve in the cold water storage tank. So she climbed into the attic with me, as I explained and showed each step of the job — down to what pipe went where, and the various fittings and joints. Her husband retreated to the living room muttering something about "leaving the girls to it."

Another woman was renovating her bathroom. She needed me to fit the bath and the toilet. But otherwise, she'd bought herself a set of pipe benders, and was making a very creative pipe run for the hot and cold taps, which she would fix to the wall. She was also going to make a vanity unit with a recycled metal bowl/sink, and do all the tiling. Having a female plumber onsite with her took the gender issue out of the equation. We were both women, both getting hands on with our tools.

In some households, it is the women who make decisions about the maintenance. In one house, I asked the man for his preferences as to how I do a task. He said he didn't know, and that I should ask his wife when she returned.

"She's the boss," he said, sloping off to his newspaper.

Some of my customers are old ladies, some of whom have been widowed, and whom are overseeing household maintenance for the first time in their lives. One such lady burst into tears on the phone when describing her broken plug hole — she was missing her husband, and was overwhelmed by her new responsibilities.

Customers want female plumbers. But businesses are slow to catch up on this. It doesn't make sense as to why more employers don't capitalise on this, and give customers what they want. Especially as the construction industry is facing a skills shortage of plumbers and gas engineers.

The workforce is ageing, and not enough young people are entering the industry to replace those retiring. There are talented women out there, who would be a huge asset to the industry.

Hiring more women would be a clever business move, if for no other reason than earning more money. A diverse workforce has been shown to reap profits, especially if they rise through the ranks to management positions. Since 2004, research organisation Catalyst found that companies with the high numbers of women in senior management performed better, with up to a third higher profits. *23. And in 2009, the Zurich-based investment firm Naissance Capital launched a $2 billion investment Women's Leadership Fund to invest in companies with women on their boards. *24.

Women have huge potential to companies. And progress — albeit slow — is being made to bring more women into the industry. These include Housing Association LiveWest, which is boosting its numbers of female trade apprentices. And one of the UK's biggest plumbing firms, Pimlico Plumbers, was on TV parading one of its apprentices — a young lady called Sophie — who spoke enthusiastically about her fledgling career.

British Gas was also actively recruiting women engineers of all ages. Even mothers who want to retrain. At the time of writing, in 2022, they were recruiting 1,000 new apprentices. Their website said that they wanted half of them to be women.

Slowly, the industry is waking up to the potential of women. Though there are stragglers. As I mentioned at the beginning of this book, in 2015, Gas Safe magazine estimated that only one percent of plumbers were female, and that just one in 300 gas engineers was a woman. *1 But precise numbers were anyone's guess, as the women weren't actually counted.

Two years later, Stopcocks tried to push this issue. "If we're not counted, do we still count?" they asked.

One of their strategies was to ask Gas Safe to include a gender tick-box on their registrations. But the response was "No." Under equal opportunities, gender apparently couldn't be highlighted on the forms. But by not counting women, how could Gas Safe monitor our needs as a group?

This information could be used to promote equal opportunities, not hinder it.

In the end, Stopcocks decided to count the women themselves. They set up the Register of Tradeswomen, which involved painstaking research of trawling through the Internet to log tradeswomen, and contacting companies. And also urging tradeswomen to get in touch, and add themselves to the register. The register also doubles-up as a database, for customers looking to hire a tradeswoman anywhere in the UK.

But as the register was launched, I wondered, did Gas Safe really want to attract more female engineers?

Each month, as a registered engineer, I receive a copy of the Gas Safe magazine, which is filled with news, technical bulletins and articles to do with gas appliances.

In September 2017, the magazine's 'star' letter sent me into a spin. I wondered if I'd gone back in time to the 1950s. The letter read:

Jobs for the Girls

I was interested to read of the initiative taken by Hattie Hasan and her pressure vehicle Stopcocks Women Plumbers (July 2017).

A few years ago, I was working at a very regular customer's house in leafy Sutton Coldfield. Mark and Penny are both very amenable and it was during another coffee break that the effervescent Penny turned to me and asked: "Rob, can I come out with you on Saturday with a view to you letting me do some plumbing?"

I readily agreed, although Mark only reluctantly gave his blessing.

The day came. Penny climbed into my van suitably attired — which I thought was a good start. We had six or seven little jobs to mop up, so we met a variety of customers. Penny quickly went into social overdrive and the customers loved her instantly, citing the fact that they felt at ease with us both and that having two dogmatic male plumbers dictating to them had, in the past, put them off from 'getting men in'.

Penny did get to fix brackets to the wall and hang a radiator in between chatting, and expressed a desire to do it again in the future. I think I'll get in touch and test her resolve.

The reality is, however, that our game can be messy and unpleasant for the best of us. Swapping a blocked-up macerator has to be up there — do the gentle sex really have the desire to get in there?

Good luck to Hattie but I do feel her slogan comes across as a tad sexist. Wouldn't something more diplomatic be preferable, such as 'Get Wimmin' In'?

Rob Cole

At first, I was furious. But I cooled down, and a few days later I emailed a response to the magazine's (female) editor. I used the tagline 'superstar letter', and continued:

Jobs for Everyone

It was interesting to read your star letter last month, in which reader Rob Cole reminisced about his day spent with an aspiring female plumber called Penny.

I too have an enjoyable day that I'd like to share, spent with my tall and muscular neighbour, Joe. He'd just left school and was looking for work. He asked if he could come out on some jobs one day. I readily agreed. Why not give him a chance, even if he is just a boy.

The day came. Joe climbed into my van. He managed not to fart or burp during the short drive to my customer's house, which I thought was a good start. We reached our first job, and Joe quickly leapt to action, removing the casing from the boiler. The customers assumed he was my boss, and chuckled merrily when I corrected them. He was, I pointed out, young enough to be my son. I told Joe that he wasn't qualified to work on gas appliances and that I was mainly a gas engineer, not a plumber. I hoped I hadn't confused him.

But he wasn't deterred. Something messy and unpleasant had caught his eye — a macerator, hooked up to the downstairs toilet. Maybe he'd like to unblock it? Within seconds, Joe was up to his elbows in excrement, with a big smile on his face.

In between his grunts, he expressed a desire to do more plumbing in the future. I think I'll get in touch. I had no idea the primitive sex enjoyed getting so dirty.

The reality is, however, that traditional women's work can also be messy. Maybe a career as a cleaner, cook, laundry worker or in an early childcare centre might appeal to Joe. Why limit his horizons?

Good luck to Rob and Penny, though I do feel his letter comes across as a tad sexist. Wouldn't something more diplomatic be preferable, such as 'Stop the stereotypes and give everyone a fair chance?'

I signed it off. Jennie Jones

A reply bounced back the same day, from the editor: Hello Jennie. Thank you so much for responding to Mr Cole's letter — I must admit, I was hoping someone would. Kind regards, Nicki.

I never imagined she'd publish the letter. It went into the next edition of the Gas Safe magazine, in the letter's section as a response to the original piece. I cried from embarrassment. I'm a quiet person who likes to live under the social radar, undetected and unseen. Yet I can't help putting myself in the spotlight.

I readied myself for angry feedback from offended readers. But none came. Either they couldn't find me online, or they all saw the funny side. Or maybe nobody even read it. Who knows?

In that same month, Stopcocks held their first Women In Trades conference in London. It was aimed at female installers, though anyone who worked or who had an interest in promoting women in the industry could attend. About 60 people attended — most of them female plumbers and gas engineers. Two had come from Ireland especially for the event. Another two had hoped to fly over from America (though bad weather had stopped their flights).

The morning was filled with talks about conflict resolution and personal branding. There were exhibits and reps from the sponsors, which included boiler, pipe and central heating companies. There was also lots of cake and opportunities to network. Stories were shared.

Hattie took the mic, and recounted her journey into plumbing. Born in the 1960s into a Turkish Cypriot family, as a girl she wasn't expected to get an education. Her mother told her that the boys wouldn't want a clever wife. Her destiny was to be a wife and mother, with no career.

But Hattie wanted a career. She initially trained to be a teacher. But a few years later, she had a change of heart. Plumbing had caught her eye.

It was the mid 1980s. The college plumbing department didn't have any female student toilets, so she had to use the staff facilities. The workshops were also full of photos of naked women, which she asked to be removed.

"I went to the department head, and asked how he thought I'd feel, knowing that I was the only one in the room with those under my t-shirt?" she told the conference. "It didn't particularly bother me personally, but it could put other women off from joining the course."

At around the same time, she wrote to every plumbing company in her area, asking to be considered for any jobs they had.

"Can you believe, not one company in Leeds was hiring plumbers?" she said.

So she bought some tools, and set out alone — with just the advice of her college tutors. I can't imagine how difficult that must have been for her. But she made a success of her jobs, and embarked on what has been a 30-year career for her.

Also during her talk, she shared some anecdotes that got other women nodding in the room. She talked about having been ignored in plumber's merchants — on one occasion, she was the only customer in the shop, yet the staff ignored her. She even called out to them: "Hello? Can I buy something?" but no joy. Or at least not until a good ten minutes had passed, and they eventually asked what she was after.

When I chatted to the other plumbers at the conference, some said they'd been asked "Who are you buying this for?" or "Who's doing the work?" I've only been asked that once, when visiting a merchant out-of-town where I wasn't known. All I can assume is that in Weymouth, the groundwork was laid by the female plumbers ahead of me.

I was glad not to have been the first female plumber in Weymouth. There was at least one very popular and talented plumber, called Becky. She could fix boilers, install bathrooms, diagnose heating faults, and even do tiling. Technically, she might have been a competitor. But I saw her as an ally, and a brilliant example of what women could achieve.

Other stories bounced around the conference. In between discussing tools and vans, and the like, the chat turned to personal safety. One of the plumbers had been groped by an elderly male customer a few weeks earlier. I wasn't told the details. He'd wanted to attend the conference, but had been told he wasn't welcome.

Another plumber recounted an incident in a narrow attic. She'd been crawling under the rafters, making her way to the cold water storage tank, when she heard a noise behind her. She looked around, and realised the customer had followed her.

"He was so close that his nose was almost touching my bum," she said.

After vocalising her surprise, she told him to back away and to get out of the attic. She had a screwdriver in her pocket, which she planned to stab him with if the situation warranted — she was that spooked. But the customer did as he was told, and no stabbing took place.

I had no such incidences to report. Other than one customer whom I suspected had a soft spot for me, whom stripped to his chest, as he changed his shirt in view of me before heading off to work.

But I took a few precautions for my safety. I always kept my online diary updated, so Stopcocks knew where I was (just in case I had an accident, fell asleep in the attic, etc). And all the customers had contacted Stopcocks to book me, so they knew that I wasn't totally out there on my own.

Rob worried for my personal safety. It was one of the first things he talked about, when I first met him, and told him about my job.

Although unusual, serious assaults on female plumbers do happen. To work alone, in a man's house, is potentially risky from that point of view. There are no guarantees of female safety. The best we can do is use our judgment — to make our excuses and leave a job if we feel worried. And many of the tradeswomen I speak to have fantasised about which tool might become an appropriate weapon, if called upon.

But most of my customers were — and still are — either female and/or old. I rarely worked for pre-retirement-aged men. So personal safety hasn't been something I worry much about.

On the flip side, a conversation I had with a drainage engineer revealed that sometimes the guys feel more at ease having a tradeswoman in their midst. If they are working in an older, single female customer's house, her presence helps everyone relax.

So women plumbers are wanted, for numerous reasons. I was in demand. Business was thriving. There were a lot of taps and toilets to fix — there always would be. A letting agent from my business networking group enlisted me to do her landlord gas safety certificates. Friends and family also booked me for work. Any hopes I had of easing myself in gently, with easier jobs, went out of the window. I had to face what came. I was under pressure to take any and all jobs.

"You can do it," said Stopcocks. "We pride ourselves on doing the jobs that others can't. Or won't. We'll help you through it."

I soon gave up on the hope of easy plumbing jobs. Anything and everything could give me grief. Even a tap change could be difficult, say if I was dealing with difficult access, and maybe rusted or tight joints. But if I didn't take on these jobs, how would I improve? I'd spent enough time in my textbooks. It was time to hit the tools.

One of my first tricky jobs was at my mother-in-law's house. She had a 40-year-old floor-standing boiler that had never been serviced. I took it apart. It then stayed in bits on the kitchen floor while I ordered a new sealing rope for the burner door.

"Don't worry about it," said Rob. "Mum's used to having stuff in bits. Sometimes it takes weeks for Dad to put things back together."

Thankfully I had their boiler back together and working after only a couple of days. Another tricky job was to change over a power shower in a friend's bathroom. It hadn't been piped up to current standards, and there was no electric switch off — it was running off the lighting circuit. She didn't want me to turn her lights off while I did the work.

After an electrician had run a new cable and fused spur to the shower, I made a start on my task. The old shower had welded itself onto the hot and cold pipes, and I couldn't pull it free. So I phoned Hattie.

"How strange," she said. "I'm doing the exact same job, and mine is also stuck. Keep at it. You'll get it off."

In the end, I took a power tool to it (my multi-tool), and cut through the plastic push-fit connections inside the shower box, taking care not to damage the water pipes (which the replacement shower would connect onto.) Mission successful, and I'd got through another job.

These days, such challenges are a routine part of my

day. I've faced so many glitches that I come to expect them. I see my job a bit like running a hurdles sprint — over one fence, and then to the next, before getting to the finish line. But back then, it was all new to me — especially the boiler maintenance.

I returned to the text books, and the boiler manuals. I spent hours poring over them. Before going on a job, I'd ask for the make/model of their boiler, or gas fire, and would read the manual from beginning to end. It was like exam time at college again, except that my exams were in the real world, and my examiner was the customer. And I needed a perfect pass.

But luckily, there was plenty of technical information at hand. Many of the boiler manufacturers run free, or low-cost, training courses on how to service their boilers. I signed myself up for them. I also made two trips to Worcester boilers, in Worcester. And a couple of trips to Ideal boilers, in Reading. And I became a regular visitor to the Vaillant training hub in Bristol.

But I still didn't feel prepared. I was terrified. Without Stopcocks pushing me on, and without the fact that I'd come so far, and had invested so much time, energy and money in my new career, I would have given up. I was out of my depth. I didn't want to give up though. And besides, what were my alternatives?

1. Work for the local newspaper (with my ex- husband as my boss).

2. A minimum-wage job in a supermarket.

I chose plumbing. But I did try to make things easier for myself, by putting the brakes on, to slow my growing business down. I gave myself more time for jobs, and more time for studying and preparing. Sometimes, I'd even do jobs for free, for the experience.

"It's my first time doing this job," I might say. "I either charge you for the job, which brings professional obligations. Or I don't charge for my labour, and you don't get a guarantee. But I get to take the stress off myself."

Customers were generally happy to be my training ground, in return for free labour. Especially as I prepared well, and did good work.

One of the best training courses I did was a professional tiling course in Hartlepool. I'd found it difficult to find a tiler to team up with on my bathroom jobs. Maybe I could do the tiling myself? So I enrolled on the course.

The course brochure, and also online reviews, said the course was 'life-changing', in that various students had picked up high-level skills that enabled them to work at a professional standard. That sounded just what I needed. What did I have to lose? Other than a huge amount of petrol, and the course fees. I booked myself on their basic, five-day course. And in January, 2018, I made the long trip up to Hartlepool.

Intense doesn't start to describe my time there. I was immersed in a packed curriculum that other colleges might take a couple of years to cover. I learned how to lay tiles, how to cut them and arrange various designs, I learned about adhesive and grout, and also about the business side to running a tiling business. It was a fantastic course.

On my last day, I bought a basic tiling kit from the college. And then I drove home, looking for my first tiling project. It didn't take me long to find something to tile. Rob's cloakroom floor was in urgent need of repair. An ongoing leak under the basin had rotted the floorboards, and also damaged a joist underneath. All this needed fixing first. And then I laid some 6mm cement board down, and then large, square, beige non-slip tiles. And then I installed a new toilet. It all looked beautiful.

Next, I tiled my first bathroom, done at no labour charge for a customer in Dorchester. They wanted an old-fashioned Victorian look, so they chose white, small rectangular tiles in a brick-wall design. I also installed my first shower tray and enclosure on that job. And I did a great job, from which I could springboard in confidence to paid tiling work.

Somehow I made it through those first two years of self-employment. I seemed to manage most of my jobs that I took on. Not all — there were a few problem jobs and customers. But in general, I got through it all OK.

I got a reputation for being a 'good plumber'. This amused me, and worried me. I didn't feel like a good plumber. I worked hard, I was intelligent, I tried to find a solution and take advice when needed. But I didn't have the experience to be 'good' at my job.

In an ideal world, I'd still have been under the supervision of an employer. I'd be sent out alone on jobs, but there would be a more experienced colleague if I needed him or her. But this isn't an ideal world. Ideals are held up to all of us — expectations of what we should be able to achieve, but they don't always take into account personal circumstances. And I was struggling to fulfil the ideals placed on me.

Not long after joining Stopcocks, I felt the conflict of my family and my work life. Stopcocks advertised themselves as a company that was open on Saturdays. But I had to look after my children at weekends. Most Saturdays, I'd be out at a football match with my youngest daughter. Jobs would come into Stopcocks, some which were emergency call-outs, and I wasn't available.

Other times, jobs would come in late afternoon during the week, and I'd already have put my tools away and collected the girls from school. I couldn't keep up with it all. So I started to block out Fridays in my online diary (alongside the Saturdays).

"I need Fridays for general stuff," I told Stopcocks. "Shopping. Housework. Catching up on things."

And that's the way it was. Naturally, my Stopcocks colleagues wanted to see my business thrive. They were well-meaning and ambitious for me. But I suspected my crazy home life was invisible to them.

My busy life also seemed to be invisible to my parents.

After a few months of running my business, I was still on a low income, with little savings, and was being propped up by benefits. After paying my plumbing overheads, I wasn't putting enough hours in to make much profit.

"It's not good to be on social handouts," my father would say.

And he was right. I didn't like it either. I was a university graduate. I never imagined I'd be in a position where I couldn't support my family. But this is where I was.

Even back then, a lot of families were struggling to pay their bills. The cost of living had already started to spiral. It usually took two incomes from both parents to sustain the household. Why did my parents think it might be achievable by one person? With such a new business? And with young children and a household to look after?

And then it dawned on me. I wasn't just a woman. I was a mother. I didn't just have 'green skin.' I had a layer of invisible 'mother' skin, which carried its own, additional challenges. I was both a female plumber and a mother. I was more unusual than I'd thought.

Chapter 13

Failure isn't an option

Anxiety is always by my side. Like my handbag. Or backpack (if I'm out plumbing.) I don't leave the house without it. And it's such a nuisance.

Having been a plumber for almost 15 years, I thought that by now, I would have conquered my nerves. That because I knew what I was doing, I could just breeze through my jobs with dazzling confidence and competence. I imagined a mental see-saw, in which as I became better at my job, my anxieties would reduce. But it hasn't worked out that way. I'm as anxious as ever. And I'm starting to think anxiety is here to stay.

Monday mornings are the worst. I lose perspective. Even a simple tap change gets me in knots. It's ridiculous. My typical Monday morning:

7.30am	My alarm goes off.
7.31am	Press snooze every 8 minutes
7.39am	I lie in bed, thinking about my jobs. I have a sinking feeling. I don't think I can do the jobs ahead of me. It's going to be a disaster. I'm going to flood the house. They'll think I don't know what I'm doing. Because I'm a woman.
7.50am	Get out of bed ten minutes early.

	My head is already in a spin.
	I wish I'd shut up.
	I just want to stop my internal chattering.
8.10am	I brush my teeth.
	More internal chatter.
	Chat, chat, chat.
	Why am I a plumber?
	I don't want to do this any more.
	Why am I even plumbing in the first place?
	Whose STUPID idea it was to retrain?
	I'm not up to this.
8.12am	I need to earn money.
	How else could I earn money?
	I don't know. I'm a useless lump.
	I have plumbing jobs booked.
	I have to go plumbing this morning.
	I can't let my customers down.
8.13am	My tummy hurts. I run to the loo.
	Am I a useless lump?
	I've been a plumber for ten years.
	I can't be that useless.
8.15am	Five trips to the loo.
	Including a last, good-luck wee.
8.45am	My head hurts.
	I do a 15-minute meditation
9.00am	Time to go to work.
	I'm exhausted by my mental shenanigans.
9.05am	One last good-luck wee.
9.10am	I sit in my van.
	I'm happy now.
	I like my van.
	I'm dressed as a plumber
	I'm surrounded by my tools, in my van.
	I feel like a plumber.
	Brum brum. Off I go.
	Maybe I can actually do this job.
	Brum brum. It might even be fun.

When I go out plumbing, I feel like it's exam day. Only I can't fail. Only perfection will do. I want to control the events that will unfold throughout the day. But plumbing isn't that predictable. Or convenient.

Customers can also be tricky. Despite me doing and saying the right things on a job, they can still get cranky — especially if they don't understand the issues I'm trying to explain. Sometimes I'm the bearer of bad news, and they unload their frustrations on to me.

So no wonder I feel anxious. And also that plumbing is widely rated as a stressful job. A survey undertaken by Ironmongery Direct and ElectricalDirect found that 74% of plumbers experience mental health issues due to their work. *25 Finances was the most common cause of stress. Workload came in at 12 percent. And — my bugbear— making mistakes was also at 12 percent.

I know that sometimes, it's impossible not to fail. I'm setting my standards too high. And I'm not doomed to fail because I am a woman. Intellectually I know all this. But my emotional side has to catch up. Failure is something I still need to learn to face. And it is the hardest thing I'll ever have to learn.

I needed help on all this. So I bought a load of self-help books, in an attempt to crack it. And I found a really great book — called How To Shine by Simon Hartley.

His book looks at people who are top of their fields, such as world-class athletes, top chefs, and the like and asks: What makes them so special? What qualities do they have that take them to the top?

I couldn't put the book down. I learned that mistakes are part of the deal. If you're pushing your limits, and stepping out of your comfort zone, you'll inevitably make mistakes. It's how we learn. But it's how we process those mistakes that makes the difference.

The world champions that Hartley writes about embrace mistakes. They look for their weak points, which they work on to improve their performance.

Two life-changing experiences greeted me when I entered plumbing college.

1. Never in my life had I pushed myself so hard.

2. It was the first time I'd had people behind me, other than my mum, who believed in me.

Plumbing isn't easy. There's a lot to learn. But because it's a hands-on, sometimes dirty job, it doesn't always get the recognition it deserves.

During one of my first afternoons at plumbing college, I made a mistake. A fitting hadn't gone together correctly. I was all fingers and thumbs in figuring it out.

"It's OK to make mistakes, Jennie,' said my tutor.

My jaw dropped. It was the first time anyone had ever said that to me.

"That's why you're here," he continued. "To make mistakes, and to learn from them. Don't worry so much."

None of my teachers at school, back in the 1980s, had ever said this to me. Instead, I was told I wasn't good enough. And likewise at university, and then with my career in journalism — I often felt held down by my bosses and colleagues, rather than being encouraged and supported up the career ladder. I was always trying to prove my worth.

Bizarrely, it was a male-dominated industry — ie, plumbing — where I was routinely told that I could 'do it', or that I'd be able to manage 'it' with time and training.

When I moved into plumbing, my confidence and self-esteem were at an all-time low. My first marriage was on the rocks. My life was at a crossroads. Little did I know what a profound effect plumbing would have on me. The comment from my new plumbing tutor came just when I most needed it.

"It's OK to make mistakes."

And it is. He was right. It's from making mistakes that we learn. But that doesn't mean it's easy to accept them. I'd prefer to learn from someone else's mistakes than my own. But life isn't always so convenient.

I read more self-help books. I found that:

1. Being out of my comfort zone will always be scary.

2. The fear is often worse than the reality.

3.The only way I'll get over my fears is by doing what I am scared of.

This was all so true. If I could, it would be better for me to take baby steps to expand my comfort zone. But I would have to take the steps, to grow — both as a plumber, and on a more personal level.

I knew I'd feel dreadful about myself if I turned away from the challenges. All the naysayers in my past would have been right about me. But I knew they were wrong. I was capable of amazing things. I had so much potential. I wanted to discover what I could achieve.

So with that in mind, I progressed through college, along my career and eventually into the arms of Stopcocks.

My new Stopcocks colleagues told me this anxiety wouldn't last forever. It was common for new plumbers to feel anxious. Mica elaborated , with another theory, which had four steps:

Step 1. In the beginning, a student doesn't know what knowledge they are missing.

Step 2. They become aware of what they don't know.

Step 3. This was the stage I was at when I joined Stopcocks. They start to pick up knowledge, and practice their new skills. They have to think everything through as they do it.

Step 4. The task becomes second nature, and doesn't demand so much of the student.

What I was feeling was completely natural. But that didn't make it any easier for me. It still doesn't.

"One day, you'll stop feeling so anxious," said Mica. "You'll start to think of yourself as a plumber and believe in your abilities. One day, you'll know you can handle anything."

"I'll look forward to that day," I replied.

But in the meantime, I needed as much support as possible. I'd be out plumbing alone. What to do if I got stuck on a job? Technical support would help. So I made a list of phone numbers of people who could give me on-the-job advice if I needed it.

Top of the list was Hattie from Stopcocks. But what if she didn't have the answers? More advisers might be needed. Such as my previous colleagues and various trade friends I'd made along the way, who I added to my list.

I could also find advice via the online forums. Some forums, especially on Facebook, can be very intimidating for newcomers. But one that I liked, and still use, is www.ukplumbersforums.co.uk The website has different sections where you can post questions ranging from taps and fittings to central heating, boilers and even insurance and job vacancies. I could post a question in the afternoon, and find a string of well-informed and friendly replies by the evening.

YouTube videos are also invaluable (as long as they are posted by experienced plumbers). More than once, I've snuck out to my van to watch a YouTube video before doing a job. As I gather, most plumbers have. But one has to be mindful of the source of the video, and that it is giving good information.

I also own lots of plumbing books and also have lots of manuals downloaded to my computer. Before a job, I ask for the make and model number of what I'll be working on. If I'm unfamiliar with it, I'll look up the manual. I like to have information at hand, if/when I need it. These days, I go to boiler jobs with my tablet in my bag. I can hook it up to the internet via my mobile phone, and then use it to download whatever manual I need.

These strategies seemed to be working. Stopcocks said they were impressed with the progress I was making. They could see me handling more complex jobs, with more confidence.

And so I stepped forward into my new career. Plumbing had so much to offer. I could work on my own terms, make good money, and do interesting and rewarding work. Just what I wanted.

Plumbing would test my confidence and resilience. I'd need to start believing in myself. And I had made progress. But the exam feeling was still with me.

It dawned on me that I might not ever leave that exam feeling, or shed the anxiety that comes with it. Maybe it was just part of the job; I'd have to learn to live with it. So with that in mind, back out I went into the big, exciting but unpredictable world of plumbing.

Chapter 14

Messing up

Guess what… I made mistakes. I can admit that now. For ages, I'd hold my head in shame. But I now see it was part of my learning curve. Embarking on such a new, challenging career was always going to be accompanied by mistakes.

It didn't take long for one of my first Stopcocks jobs to go wrong. My task had been to replace the basin taps on a 20-year-old vanity unit. The customer had already chosen and bought the taps. It should have been an easy job, but — as can easily happen with plumbing — pre-existing issues made the job more complicated.

In this case, the tap connections under the sink had been leaking for some time. There was significant rust, that made it impossible to undo the connections.

I was at a crossroads. By this stage, I'd already turned the water off, and had cut the pipes. Should I look like an idiot and back out of the job? Or should I crack on with it. Because I had started the work, I felt that I had to complete the job, come what may.

I decided to remove the basin, soak the connections in a lubricant, and try again. So I explained this to the customer, and warned them of a risk of damage — as, obviously, porcelain sinks are fragile. They said to go ahead and do what needed to be done. In retrospect, I should have got their permission in writing. But I didn't.

It was only verbal.

So I continued the work, feeling uneasy. Nevertheless, I carried on. Out came the basin. I then managed to get the old taps off, albeit with some difficulty. I could never have got them off in situ.

But my lack of experience showed. I hadn't realised the fragility of the surface of the vanity unit. Around the surfaces where I had prised the basin off from, the laminate fascia had started to pull away from the chipboard unit. I re-fitted the basin, and tried to glue the rips down. Albeit small, they were visible, and my patch-up attempt couldn't undo the damage.

The customer wasn't happy. They declared it to be an "insurance job." The vanity unit was part of a larger, bespoke built in sink/cupboard/worktop unit. They wanted it all replaced, and a matching bath panel fitted. This would be the only resolution, they announced.

I gave them details of my insurance company, who requested photos and a description of the damage from the customer. I was no longer in the loop. I assumed an assessor would come out, to inspect the damage in person. Or that I'd be asked to confirm — or deny — the extent of what damage I'd caused, and what may have been pre-existing. But this didn't happen either. The insurance company paid for a new bathroom. And I received a bill for £500 of excess insurance payment, for what had only been a £60 job.

Stopcocks were furious with the insurance company. And I felt terrible. But I learned a lot from the experience. First, I learned about the fragility of bathroom units. But more importantly, I learned to trust my instincts. If a job looks problematic, the issues need to be discussed with the customer. And if I still feel uneasy, maybe I should turn the job down.

Surely better I sometimes say the job is too difficult for me than put myself under undue stress. I needed to be challenged, but not be out of my depth. If I was going to make mistakes, I wanted to soften the blows. There was still a huge amount of learning ahead of me.

One is always learning — even 60-year-old plumbing veterans say that every day is a 'school day.' But I still had to learn and practice the basics. I didn't need to master it all immediately. Some jobs would be best declined. The day would come when I'd be better able to face them. They'd be a battle for another day.

And so began a tug of war with Stopcocks. As jobs began to roll in, most of them I could take on, especially with their encouragement and technical support. But some jobs needed on-site assistance, which — being based in Yorkshire — they couldn't give me.

A request for underfloor heating came in. Underfloor heating was a specialism that I had little knowledge, and no experience of. The closest I'd come to it was a study module at college. So no, I wasn't going to take that job on.

Not long after, another difficult tap job came up. The customer wanted me to replace an expensive, tall kitchen tap that was mounted directly onto a wooden worktop. Access was difficult. But getting a tool to fit the back-nut was impossible. None of my tools would fit.

I drove around the merchants, to see what they had. Nothing they sold would fit either. I figured that I could force the back-nut off. Or cut it off. But I could end up in no man's land with a loose tap that I still couldn't remove. Or a damaged worktop. This job didn't feel good.

"Keep trying," said Stopcocks.

"I could spend the next week trying, and it still won't come off," I said. "How long do you expect me to lie under their worktop for? I don't have a tool to fit. And besides, I have to pick the kids up from school in two hours."

These days, I have a very expensive tap removal kit that may have done the job. But I wasn't ready for that job at the time, and walking away was the right decision that day. And so I apologised to the customer, saying it was a job I couldn't do. I left the tap as found.

That second tap was a turning point. If I didn't want to take on a job, I decided that I wouldn't. Though I'd need to be honest with myself why. Was it fear? Or were there technical or practical reasons that I couldn't overcome?

Finding this balance has always been a challenge for me, as I'm prone to snap judgements in which I declare a job too difficult for me. Sometimes, I later think "Oh, maybe I could have done that after all."

There were plenty of times that I needed a nudge from Stopcocks to get me out there. Without them, I would have stayed home, curled up on my sofa in despair. But over time, there was a shift in my thoughts. I started to relax. And as I relaxed, I could think more clearly, and do my work better.

And I also became more open to taking on challenging jobs. For example, I used to worry about boiler breakdowns. I used to be terrified of going out to them. Sometimes I still am. But then I became curious. I wanted to see what the fault might be. And if I couldn't get to the job, I'd be disappointed — like I'd missed out on something fun.

So I found a solution. I was going to have to be kind to myself. I would have to find my limits and be mindful of what jobs I could take. The world wouldn't always understand. But if I didn't do this, I risked burning out — both mentally and physically.

If I was careful not to over-stretch my limits, my anxiety might subside. And when I'd inevitably make mistakes, I might be in a better position to deal with the fallout.

Chapter 15

An inspector calls

Gas safety is a big deal. For obvious reasons. I'd been qualified as a gas engineer for two years when I received an email from Gas Safe. They wanted to inspect my work. Not because I'd done shoddy work, but as part of a general check on new engineers.

The email gave a proposed date for the inspection, but I would be away on holiday. I phoned them straight back, to let them know. But as luck would have it, the assessor was in Weymouth that day. Maybe he could visit me that afternoon? I happened to be free, so I said yes. I wanted to get it over and done with.

Ideally, I would have lined up house visits to three customers. But due to the late notice, that wouldn't be a problem. He'd test me on the boiler in the house I rented.

And so it was that the inspector turned up in my house. He was older — late 50s — with white hair, short, a little tubby, and a friendly smile. After introducing himself, his first words were: "Are you nervous?"

"Yes, I am," I replied.

He assured me I needn't be. I should have been visited by Gas Safe months earlier, when I'd emerged from my six-month probation period (i.e., only working under supervision from a more experienced engineer.) However, there had been a backlog of work for the assessors. So now that he was back in Weymouth, first-timers — like myself — were on the list for a visit. I was happy with that. I wanted to confirm that I was working safely. We had the same goals.

First, he asked how I should test my home for a gas leak — done via a manometer, at my gas meter. Not long before, there had been a leak. I'd smelt gas, and found the leak at the test nipple on the meter. The gas supplier had been out, and the meter was fixed. So I was confident there wouldn't be any issues with that test.

And then we ran through the boiler checks, using my flue gas analyser to measure the exhaust gases from the boiler. And then a cup of tea, and some theory. He wanted some fireplace measurements I couldn't remember off the top of my head, such as the minimum thickness of a gas hearth. I keep books in my van, so I can look up such things as needed. So out came the books.

I was starting to enjoy myself. He asked if I had any questions. Where to start? I had loads of questions. Things I'd debated with colleagues, and wanted to confirm.

"Do you have to be a Gas Safe engineer to change a boiler pressure relief valve?" Yes. I'd thought so.

"Does a broken pressure relief valve mean the boiler becomes 'At Risk' and should be turned off?"

Yes. I knew it. Granted, it was detailed in my plumbing gas book. But I'd come into conflict with a customer over that one. Having it confirmed made me appear less of a stickler for stubbornly following rules. But had that boiler exploded off the wall, I've no doubt they would have thrown the rules back at me with enthusiasm.

So that was that. I'd passed my inspection. And he was off (after first giving me his phone number to add to my list of technical advisers). And I'd passed. PASSED. That meant my initial ACS (gas) exams hadn't been a lucky fluke. It had just been re-confirmed. I was a Gas Safe registered engineer, tested. Twice. And so I took another step forward into my new career.

Chapter 16

The tipping point

It had been a big day, followed by an even bigger evening. I was dizzy from all the alcohol I'd consumed. I'd had two halves of lager, and about four glasses of wine. This was a huge amount of alcohol for me. It was the most I'd drunk in a single evening for years. And I was having fun. As I always did when I went to Stopcocks meet-ups.

It was early September. We'd met in Coventry, for the annual Installers convention. The day-time featured plumbing demonstrations and talks, and lots of trade stands. That evening, we attended the Installers fundraiser dinner, at which Stopcocks received an award for their services to plumbing. Afterwards, some of our group ventured off to the onsite casino. I opted to join the 'cup of tea' group, who had gone up to a hotel room to wind down for the night.

I got chatting to Mica, asking her about her days as a protester at the Greenham camp in the 1980s. She was one of around 30 women to live at the camp.

She told me about the daily chores, of cooking food, cleaning clothes, sanitation. And she also told me about the protests against the American missiles, about how she dressed as a bunny to climb the Greenham Common perimeter fence. And also about how a baby was born at the camp. I was fascinated.

During the four years I spent with Stopcocks, we

had numerous get-togethers. And I loved those times. We always had a lot to talk about. Other get-togethers included a tour around a plumbing pipe/fitting factory, and a two-day course on underfloor heating. I also went on a two-day LPG gas course, organised through Stopcocks.

Other times, at our meetings, we'd discuss plumbing news and issues, or be visited by reps from boiler companies, who would show us their products. Or maybe we'd sit through a training session led by Stopcocks, if there was an issue we all needed advice on.

On top of that, an annual conference for women plumbers was also started up by Stopcocks. The first one was held in 2017. Typically, they feature a morning of inspirational and informative talks, lunch, and a networking session. Delegates started to get to know each other. Friendships were made, and a national community of female plumbers started to build.

I loved being part of Stopcocks, and the wider community of female plumbers. I didn't want to go out plumbing on my own. Thanks to social media, and mobile phones, I could always be connected to a larger group of women plumbers. But this wouldn't last forever. I always knew it wouldn't. The day would come when I'd decide to leave Stopcocks.

I assumed that it would be a financial decision. For in addition to paying a monthly fee, I was also adding ten percent on my labour invoices to give to Stopcocks.

This was quite a hit on my income. Though in those early days of self-employment, the fees weren't such an issue. Tax credits and other social security benefits buoyed me up. This gave me time to focus on my skills and confidence, without the extra pressure on a fledgling business to cover all my family's living costs.

Though the day would come when I'd need to be financially self-sufficient. I didn't want to depend on benefits forever. And to achieve that, I'd need to be much tighter about my business overheads, such as my Stopcocks fees.

But in the end, I left for other reasons. It was a decision that was brewing for months, but in the end, it was made quickly, over Christmas 2019. This was how it happened.

A couple of months before, in late November of that year, I had been visited by my new landlady. Her father had died the year before, and she'd inherited the house I rented — a three-bedroom semi-detached former council house.

"I'm afraid I have some bad news," she'd said.

She was planning to sell up, and use the money to move to Blackpool. She wanted to give me plenty of notice, so I'd had a chance to find another home. Or apply for a mortgage — if I wanted, I'd have first dibs on buying this house. But I didn't have that kind of money. So she advised I start looking for somewhere else to live.

Me and the girls adored the house. We didn't want to move out.

"We live like queens here," I used to tell the girls.

As a single mum on a low income, I'd been extremely lucky to get that house. And as rents had increased over the years, her father hadn't increased it. But my chances of affording another home like this were minimal.

Though I wasn't as upset as I might had been, as I knew this day would come. It always did.

I'd been living in this house for eight years. My previous tenancy record was only three years with my previous homes. Eventually, the owners had always wanted their properties back — either to live in themselves, or to sell. So I'd always thought of that house as temporary.

"If you can't find anywhere else to live, I might be able to re-mortgage this house for a year," she said. "To give you more time."

She was the nicest landlady I'd ever had. So as we stood in my kitchen drinking tea, with my eight-week-old kitten Bella perched on her shoulder, I told her she wouldn't need to do that. I already had plans. For the last couple of years, Rob and I had been talking about living together. The plan was for me and the girls to move in with him. And to also get married.

"You've given us a nudge to get on with it," I said. "We've been planning this for ages. But we've got a lot of work to do on his house. I don't know if we could make it happen without this kind of a push."

We agreed on a three-month notice period. That wasn't long, though more than I was legally entitled to. But the clock was still ticking.

I had so much work to do — both in clearing out and cleaning my current home, and in finishing the renovations on Rob's house before we could move in. Rob's house still needed a lot of work before we could comfortably move in. After years of neglect, most of the house needed attention.

The previous summer I'd started work to renovate his kitchen. I'd ripped out the old units, and tiled the kitchen floor and splashbacks. I'd then fitted the new (secondhand) units, sink and taps.

And I'd finally re-painted the walls, and put some blinds on the window. I'd also previously renovated the upstairs bathroom. It had new tiled walls, a new (secondhand) corner bath, and a new toilet. Both rooms looked awesome. But so much more work needed to be done on the rest of the house.

The biggest challenge was to create a fourth bedroom somewhere, as none of the upstairs bedrooms were big enough for the girls to share. So we planned to put a stud wall at the end of the living room, and make a small bedroom for Rob's then 18-year-old son.

"This might not be done before you move in," said Rob, who was working full-time and didn't have enough spare time to take on such a project. But if it wasn't done now, when would it be done? Would it ever be done? Possibly not.

"I want our family to be happy," I said. "We won't be happy if we're wedged in here, living like squatters. So the fourth bedroom needs to be sorted."

Regardless, fourth bedroom or not, the girls and I were going to move in with Rob. I shared the news with my parents. This was big news. My mother was concerned.

"Why don't you get your own place?" she asked. "Keep your independence. Women don't need men to survive."

This came from someone who had been married for more than 40 years. I tried to explain that I didn't want to do all this alone. I didn't want to wash up alone. To mow the lawn alone. To wake up alone (on the weekends that Rob wasn't with me). I wanted a future with Rob in it.

"Are you telling me a plumber can't earn enough to support his/her family?" she asked. "Single mums are strong — they can have careers and still be mums."

Yet again, I was sick of being told that single mothers could 'do it all'. I'd tried, and I couldn't manage it all. Some mothers may have careers that pay enough to support their families financially. Some even have money left over to pay for cleaners and other domestic help (if they don't have time to do it themselves). I'm friends with some of them.

But this isn't generally the case. A study in 2019 found that 49% of single parents — the vast majority (90%) of whom were women — were living in poverty. *26 and *27. When I am told that single mothers should be able to support themselves and their families financially, I see a society that is failing to look after its most vulnerable members.

I earned good money when I went plumbing, but I wasn't rich. I was shocked by how much unpaid work (i.e., paperwork, estimates, buying materials, job research and planning) took up time. As well as overheads to pay, such as van maintenance, insurance, buying tools, Gas Safe registrations, etc.

When I wasn't plumbing, I was immersed in childcare, housework, shopping, cooking, gardening, driving the girls to the various clubs, and so on. My life was hectic, and exhausting.

Rob was in awe of how much I had done and achieved.

But while I did so much, I still didn't do enough. I was limited in how much time and effort I could put into my plumbing business. I felt so overwhelmed by all my responsibilities. There wasn't enough of me to do all this alone. My mother was wrong — at least about my family life. When children are on the scene, men are very much needed.

And I didn't just need Rob. I wanted him. I didn't want to be alone. I wanted to be part of a team — me and him facing the world, and all its challenges, together. We were going to make this happen. We would renovate his house, and turn it into a comfortable, family home we could thrive in. But I'd need to throw all my efforts into it. The challenge was on. And I needed time to do this.

Thankfully, that year I'd already blocked out a couple of weeks before Christmas to finish the kitchen renovations. And so far, I'd only booked a handful of small plumbing jobs for the New Year. My diary was relatively free, which was unusual, as I was often booked up for weeks. At the time, Stopcocks were sometimes taking up to seven calls a day for me, from both existing and prospective customers. I couldn't keep up with it all.

Every so often, I'd ask Stopcocks that no new customers be taken on for a few weeks, until I'd dealt with my current jobs. I'd have to do this again. So I phoned Stopcocks, and told them about my impending eviction, and that I'd need more time to work on Rob's house.

"Please don't send me any new customers," I said. "And with existing customers, anything that isn't urgent, I'll put off until after Christmas."

A couple of days later, I received an email from Stopcocks detailing a plumbing job in my street. A new customer, who had just moved in, needed a washing machine to be plumbed in. There was some kind of issue around this being done, but I forget the details. But I stared at the email. There was so much work to be done at Rob's house. How was I going to make time for even this supposedly smallest of jobs? I phoned them up, to say

I couldn't take that job. I was too busy. Flat out. So I said no. They'd need to cancel the customer. And that was that.

No more plumbing jobs came through, and I continued with my renovations. And I was unstoppable. I loved sorting Rob's house out. Yes, it was a lot of work. But it was for us, and for our future as a family. I was at his house every day, busy at various tasks.

First, I emptied and decorated the third, smaller bedroom. I figured that completing one room would lead the way for the rest of the house. This would be the bedroom for my eldest daughter, who was then aged 11. But there was a hitch — I didn't know how to wallpaper. Some lessons would be needed. Rob demonstrated how it should be done. And then I sent him out the room.

"Why can't I watch?" he asked.

"You'll find it too painful," I said. He was already banned from watching me cut wood with a saw. "If I need you, I know where you are."

He'd been a good teacher. I seemed to get good results. Or most of the time anyway. I also found that I enjoyed wallpapering. I found it relaxing.

I put plain wallpaper up in my first bedroom, and painted it a light peach colour. And I painted the skirting boards/window ledge in white gloss. I bought new curtains, and put up shelves. And I finally put the bed and furniture back in.

My daughters loved the room. From then on, when we went to visit (but before moving in), the girls sat in the room and played on their tablets. I told Rob they were like ferrets down a hole.

'Teenagers like being in their bedrooms,' I announced. He already knew this, having already brought up two sons.

Christmas was coming. I painted the stair banisters, cleared bags and bags of clutter from the living room, and unearthed the dining table, that had been lost under heaps of stuff for the last few years.

All too soon, there were only two days left before

Christmas Day. Time had run away with me. I hadn't yet bought a Christmas tree.

I drove around the shops — everywhere had sold out, except for B&Q, who had a couple left on clearance, for £1 each. I bought one of the trees, and put it in Rob's living room. I also cleared the seating area and put up some decorations. And we were ready for Christmas.

Meeting this festive challenge was really important to us. Not only would we have a nice space to use, but it would also show us that we could meet the challenge of sorting out the rest of the house. That we were masters of our destiny. That this huge task ahead of us might just be possible. And then I received a phone call from Stopcocks.

They were worried that I wasn't earning enough money from my business. But it was bad timing. I flipped. How dare they suggest I should be putting in more hours, and reaping more profit. Wasn't I already doing enough in my life?

Stopcocks have since told me that it wasn't their intention to put me under any pressure. They just wanted to help me, and to see me and my business thrive. Likely, I misinterpreted their call. After all, us humans are prone to misunderstandings, especially in phone calls and emails.

But I'd already decided before the phone call that the time had come for me to leave Stopcocks. My business was growing faster than I could cope with. Stopcocks were doing their best to propel me forwards, and I was pushing backwards. We had different needs, and different goals. We were going in different directions.

And as I thought more about it, I realised how I'd taken to heart what the world said I should achieve. So many people were full of advice and opinions about how I should be living. But none of them understood my challenges, or knew what was best for me. The best person to run my life was me. And that would entail leaving Stopcocks, so I could better manage my work/life balance.

I considered how far I'd come. I'd evolved as a plumber,

and also as a person. I could finally stand strong, on my own out there. I just about had the experience and the confidence to finally be self-employed.

A busy Christmas was ahead of me. I looked into setting up under my own name. I'd need a website, an online accounts/diary/database package, and business cards. None of this would be difficult to sort out. I'd be OK. I could do this.

So much change. In such a short time. And with leaving Stopcocks, I felt a new kind of freedom, like a kid leaving home for the first time. It was scary, but something I wanted to embrace. I spent that Christmas full of smiles, and skipping around Rob's house in delight. A new year was coming, and with it so much change. I was so excited.

Chapter 17

Living through covid

I felt guilty. But also very happy. It was Rob's birthday. March 16, 2020. He'd taken the day off work to celebrate, only we didn't get the chance.

We spent the morning stripping wallpaper, and were looking forward to going out for lunch with his parents — possibly to a small pub in Portland, with views over Chesil Beach. That would do beautifully. But lunch didn't happen.

For the last few weeks, we'd watched news of the Covid pandemic as it swept across the world, creating chaos as it went. We watched news reports of lockdowns and struggling hospitals in Italy. And now the virus was in the UK.

Kids were being taken out of schools (which would soon close, anyway). And Rob's parents were frightened. They daren't leave their house. And neither could we go to see them. Vulnerable people — such as the elderly — had already been advised to 'shield.'

"That's a shame," we thought. "Let's crack on with the DIY, and we'll go out this evening instead. Just the two of us."

At some point, we nipped out to the local supermarket for supplies. We bumped into one of Rob's friends in the car park, who felt that we were all overreacting.

"Covid isn't in Weymouth," he announced.

But it was. And with it was a lot of confusion and worry.

The various lockdowns had yet to be implemented. But by mid-afternoon, many of the nation's pubs and restaurants had already shut. So we settled for a take-away, and a movie on the TV.

Already that week, we had watched the first of many TV government press conferences, detailing the spread and nature of the virus. As the virus hit Italy, I suspected we wouldn't be far behind, and that I might not be able to shop for my various DIY materials. So I'd hurriedly ordered a garden shed, paving stones and gravel, paint, wallpaper and a carpet for our bedroom. There was a constant stream of deliveries. It was like living in a warehouse.

Rob's kitchen had just been finished, complete with a new gas hob. I hadn't been happy with the old hob.

"I'm not living with that," I'd announced, pointing at its cracked top, and absence of safety devices that would check the flame hadn't gone out. So I'd fitted a new one.

Typical to Rob's house, the job had become bigger. The previous installer cut the square recess in the worktop too big. I'd bought a same-sized hob. But as luck would have it, Rob had a spare worktop in the shed. So I installed a new worktop with the hob.

By then, the fourth bedroom had also been built. The two of us had erected a timber frame. I'd then fixed up the plasterboard walls, and wallpapered them. I left the door for Rob to hang.

Throughout all this, we watched the news. Covid was the only news story. We watched as social distancing laws came in. One of these laws was a ban on the mixing of households. Technically, Rob and I shouldn't see each other. We should stay in our separate homes.

But this had practical difficulties for me. I had already started to move in with Rob. I'd begun to sell my surplus furniture. I'd sold the washing machine, and had installed my dishwasher and tumble dryer in Rob's kitchen. The girls bed frames had been moved across town as well.

But we couldn't yet sleep at Rob's house, because

I had a six-month-old kitten. I couldn't yet take her to live at Rob's, as it wasn't safe or secure for her. So the girls and I were sleeping on mattresses on the floor of our old house, in sleeping bags.

I was in limbo. We decided that — under the circumstances — we were already a household. We'd already partially combined our households. So I continued with the renovations and the move.

When the schools closed, I juggled homeschooling with the renovations. My eldest daughter was very organised with her work, and didn't need much supervision. But the youngest would fly through her work in under an hour. Comments would come back from her teacher.

"It isn't a race," he'd say.

And I'd encourage her to take more care over her work. Sometimes I'd sit down with her, and go through the work with her. But it was a struggle. She wanted to be left to her own devices.

While the nation talked about coping strategies for loneliness and boredom — such as taking up new hobbies, or YouTube fitness videos — I was even more immersed in my renovations. For despite home-schooling the girls, I had more time to concentrate on the move.

Meanwhile, Rob was still going work. There had been the option for him to stay home due to possible health vulnerabilities to the virus — ie, his age and weight. But he asked to be put on outside, solitary tasks.

"People need their phone lines," we figured. This was a time that we must pull together as a nation, and all do our bit. So off to work he went.

And then some good news. Or at least, good for us. An extension on my moving date was given to me by my landlady, as the house sale had fallen through.

"We're not going to be able to sell it until after the lockdowns, so you might as well stay in the house a bit longer," she said.

"It would only be sitting empty otherwise."

I ended up with an extra six weeks. And they ended up being some of the happiest weeks of my life. As well as the most stressful. It was a strange time.

As summer arrived, the weather was glorious. During those weeks, we fell into a new routine.

On the weeks the girls were with me (sometimes they'd be with their dad), they'd spend the morning studying. Afternoons would be spent on art/crafts or reading. Or an online activity or lesson (a load of websites offering lessons sprang up almost overnight, albeit at a cost).

I spent hours outside playing with the girls, particularly with my youngest daughter. I bought a paddling pool, a swing ball set and a badminton net, which I put up in our back garden. We also played football in the nearby park, and also spent hours shooting a ball into the basketball hoop (which, not having a fence around it, hadn't been possible for the council to close).

"It's like being on holiday," she said.

I was glad, as her happiness was of utmost importance. Those weeks became a special time for us. Although it was with relief that primary schools later took Year 6 students back for the last few weeks of the summer term.

But I felt guilty, because the lockdowns had come as a relief. I needed the time for the house move. While other people's lives were on hold, and they were worrying about their jobs, security, and even their lives, I was literally busy building my future.

There was still a lot of work to do. I started to lay the foundations for a new shed at the end of the garden. I was also going to lay a path down the garden to it. I laid out a snake of paving stones — each morning, I would set three more of them into the lawn. It started to take shape.

Sometimes the girls would help me. They enjoyed pulling old wallpaper off, and painting the walls, and clearing the garden of brambles. One afternoon, they even helped me build the shed. One of them held a spirit level, and the other held the relevant shed panel, while

I screwed the shed together. Across the next-door gardens, I was aware of the neighbours watching as we put the roof on. Thankfully it didn't fall off. We fitted it without any issues.

We were making progress. But I was working hard. Too hard. I started to feel the strain.

Chapter 18

The cracks start to show

Something had to give. I was working so hard. Too hard. It wasn't a fitting that exploded, or a shelf that fell down, or the like. Nope. Something much worse. In the end, it was me that fell apart. By the time I realised the stress was getting to me, it was too late. I'd been pushing myself too hard for too long. And even when I first started feeling stressed, I still didn't slow down.

During the first Covid lockdowns, I was still spending every day doing Rob's house up. Evenings were spent packing, and clearing my old house out. And this was in addition to home-schooling and playing with my kids, and general household chores. I felt overwhelmed. I sketched a timetable for my various jobs. It was ambitious. But I was determined to do it.

And while I was enjoying seeing my new life and home coming together, I was up against the clock. Despite my moving out date being put back, there was still so much to do in such a short time.

Every two weeks, the girls went to stay with their dad (they yo-yo'd between us during the lockdowns).

I went home one kid-free afternoon, and flopped down on the sofa. The house was so quiet, and so still. I'd be seeing Rob later, but he likely wouldn't be around until late evening. I suddenly felt so alone.

But I wasn't alone. Bella, the kitten, was delighted that

I was home. I was tired, and I shut my eyes. I hoped to take a nap. But Bella didn't want me to. She didn't like my eyes being shut, and she licked my face until I gave up on sleep. She then sat on the back of my neck, and purred.

I could no longer whimper about being alone. Her company was wonderful. She was so comforting. I loved her so much. She was the first cat that I had owned. Such moments with her were so precious, especially during the lockdowns. We were so lucky to have her in our lives.

The moment of sadness passed. But later, it returned. I was stewing over a disagreement I'd had with Rob. He'd dared to criticise my workmanship with a section of wallpapering in our bedroom. I'd hit the roof. How dare he nitpick my efforts? I was doing my best. I wasn't a professional decorator. He should consider himself lucky I was having a go at such tasks.

I was also scared about the move. I had a failed marriage behind me. Was I doing the right thing? Would we be happy together? Would our kids be happy? I was also sad to say goodbye to the house I'd lived in all these years. I'd known this time would come, that I couldn't hang on to a rented house forever. But it was still a wrench. It had been a fantastic home for me and the children.

The backdrop to all this was the Covid pandemic, which was then claiming around 1,000 lives a day. Would my family, my friends, and myself be OK? Would we make it out the other side in one piece?

My life suddenly felt out of control. Like I was in a car, that was picking up speed, but I didn't know where the brakes were. And I needed someone to hold me still, to tell me it would all be OK. But there was no one. We were in lockdown.

So I just carried on ruminating. The list of worries grew. I was worried about money, worried about if I still had any friends (no one ever phoned or messaged me), worried about not keeping up with my knee physio (would I end up back on crutches?)

And now I was worried about how much I was worrying. I had so much on my mind.

I hadn't realised how the stress was getting to me. Despite repeated warnings on the TV about looking after one's mental health, I didn't see this coming. I'd buried my worries. But they had emerged, punching their way into the world like fireworks.

I needed cheering up. So I turned the TV on, and opened a bottle of Prosecco. I drank my first glass. The liquid was cold, and bubbly. It was delicious. And also very easy to drink. It went down too easily.

With no one to share the bottle with, it wasn't long before I'd drank more than half of it. I was drunk. It had been years — before my kids were born — since I'd been so tipsy. The room was spinning. My mind felt still, and logical, while the world span around me. So I drank another glass, and finally fell asleep on the sofa, with the kitten still perched on my neck.

Sometime later that evening, Rob let himself in. He had a key. He came round most evenings. I was still asleep on the sofa, but the cat heard him arrive. As he stepped into the house, she slipped through his legs, and out into the night. This was a bad thing. She was too young to be outside on her own. Rob followed her into the street. He found her sitting under a car, where she hissed at another cat. And then she was off again, and sat in the middle of the road, looking up at him. When he tried to pick her up, she swiped at him, cutting his hand.

He came back into the house and woke me up. Why was I so drunk? I was needed. I hoisted myself up, and went outside. The cat was still sitting in the road. If she couldn't be picked up, I'd have to lure her back. So I fetched her cat toy — a rod, with dangly feathers. And I swished it in front of her playfully. She couldn't resist it. She jumped up, and was immersed in the game.

I skipped back to the house, waving it in front of her. The little cat skipped happily behind me, trying to get the feathers. And when we reached the front of the house, she just stood there. I picked her up, took her indoors, and shut the door behind us. And then I collapsed back on the sofa, and fell instantly asleep again.

The next morning, I felt shaky and sick — a classic hangover. And Rob was concerned. The stress was getting to me. I wasn't invincible. He wanted me to go to the doctor and get anti-depressants or whatever medication might stabilise me. But I didn't feel depressed. Just very stressed.

"I've been trying to do too much," I said. "I need to slow down. Giving me tablets so I can keep working so hard is sick. No tablets. I need to address the underlying cause behind the stress."

While medication is a life-saver for a lot of people, I recognised the effect the stress and the long hours had had on me. I'm prone to working too hard, and not taking enough time to recharge. I would try to manage the stress in other ways. But some help in doing so would be invaluable.

I went online. I found a Dorset-based health organisation that focused on well-being — such as weight loss, giving up smoking, and mental health issues such as stress and depression. I didn't need a referral. I could just fill in their online questionnaire, and they'd take it from there. This I did. And the next day, they phoned me — initially to check I wasn't suicidal. They didn't beat about the bush.

"Why are you still here?" they asked.

"I've got children?" I answered it as more of a question than an answer. And then I relaxed. "I like being here. I don't want to leave."

Having got that out of the way, they arranged another day/time for a more in-depth phone consultation, where I could talk about my problems to a counsellor.

And so it was that I described my life and worries to a stranger on the phone. He said he was about my age, and understood the pressures I was under. He recommended I attend an eight-week webinar about stress management that his organisation ran. It would be run over video calls online. I'd log on Wednesday mornings for eight weeks, and join a virtual classroom with other clients, and learn all about stress management.

I was stunned. They had dedicated an entire course to stress. I'd only previously heard about depression, and other mental health issues. But not stress. I'd not realised it was such a big deal.

A couple of weeks later, I logged on for my first webinar. Two tutors, working from their home offices (i.e., living rooms), came online. About 30 students were also online, unseen but listening.

The first session looked at what stress was. What could trigger it? What did it feel like? I was stunned to see all the comments that flooded into the classroom's chat box. I read about how other students felt overwhelmed and unable to meet demands, and felt they weren't doing enough. These people were like me. These feelings were common.

Would other sessions be so informative? I looked forward to learning more. Those Wednesdays became a highlight of my week, in which I felt reconnected to people in the outside world, and also empowered by what I was learning.

Other sessions looked at healthy living, such as diet, exercise, sleep, and excessive caffeine or alcohol. And how to break down challenges into more manageable chunks, to be more realistic in what we expect from ourselves, and some meditation and relaxation techniques.

I also started to unpick the sources of my stress. Underneath it all was my fear of plumbing. My workplace worries topped the scale in the various questionnaires we filled in. It wasn't the only trigger. But it was a significant one. I might have been taking a couple of months out from my plumbing. But it was still in my head. The little voice, saying: 'What if you can't cope?' still plagued me.

Through the course, I learned to face those fears better. I learned that the fear was far worse than anything

I could ever face on a job. To hide from my fears would make them more potent. And in turn, I'd lose confidence and feel disempowered.

I also learned more about the benefits of meditation. I learned that it's natural for our minds to be busy. But just taking a few minutes to be still, to try to quell the internal chatter, is so helpful. It is like pressing a 'pause' button. The vortex of thoughts and emotions loses its energy. And I'd emerge feeling a bit more able to face the world.

When I'd eventually go back to work, it would be without Stopcocks. But I'd have to be mindful about what jobs I'd take on. Plumbing can be a stressful job. If I took care not to overload myself, and to better look after myself, I could better cope with the more challenging jobs that came along.

In the years since I'd taken up plumbing, I'd been trying to fit in with other people's ideals of how I should be working. There had been no shortage of opinions as to how I should be growing my business. Which — as I could see — sometimes pained outsiders, as I had a business that had a fantastic demand and great money-making potential.

"Take on help," they'd say. "You need an apprentice. Or a partner. Or office support."

But I didn't want any of these things. I didn't want the responsibility of having an apprentice or a business partner. Nor the obligation to put in the hours and effort that I'd owe such people. I figured that if I needed an extra pair of hands, I could simply pay for an appropriate person to do what needed doing.

If I'd wanted to, I could have grown my business. I could have sought investors, taken on staff. It might have been fun. But I didn't want to take it to those heights. I wanted to keep it small. I didn't want the stress or responsibility, or hours, that such a business would need from me.

I needed autonomy, and to be able to work in ways that suited myself. So a change of approach would be required. When the lockdowns eased, I'd go back out plumbing. But it would be on my own terms. Only I could figure out the best way forward. And that was what I would do.

Chapter 19

Would I do it again?

Would I do it again? Did I make the right choice to retrain as a plumber? I don't know. That's not an easy question to answer. Like most things in life, there are pros and cons to the path I've chosen.

I seem to have mastered the basics of what I do. Another gas refresher course has been and gone (the exams need to be re-sat every five years). I now take on bigger jobs — such as bathroom renovations, and upgrading heating systems from old back boilers to new combination boilers. And I take on more boiler repairs. There's still a lot to learn. There always will be. But I'm more on top of things now.

But one of my top worries is that I won't be able to do this work until retirement. Plumbing is a tough physical job that requires strength and fitness.

I'm not at my physical prime anymore, and certainly won't be at the age of 67 (the current retirement age for my generation). So if I can't go out plumbing, what will I do for money? That worries me. Maybe I should have picked a career with a longer shelf-life.

As I finish this book, in the summer of 2022, I've just passed my 50th birthday. I hate to admit it, but I'm starting to feel my age. I get tired more easily. There was once a time that I could party all night, and still go to work the next day. Those days have gone. I now need a solid eight hours of sleep just to cope with the most basic of days.

Sometimes I'm so tired that I could crawl under a bath and fall asleep at work. With back-to-back days of plumbing and family demands, finding recovery time is difficult. Ultimately, I fall apart. I call it an 'energy crash'. I've had some weekends where I couldn't get out of bed for exhaustion.

"What's wrong with me?" I ask. "The rest of the world goes out and does a full-time job. Why can't I?"

But I know that's not the case. I know people with physical disabilities and needs that makes it near-on impossible for them to pursue a regular 40-hour work week. One woman I know suffers from MS (the yuppie flu). She describes her energy as being like 'packets of energy.' She can only use so many packets per day, and then she needs to rest. If she over-spends, she'll suffer extreme exhaustion for days.

Sometimes I chat to the older women I meet at the gym. One woman, in her 60s, tells me about her husband, who is a mechanic. His boss expects him to put in the same physical effort as his colleagues in their 20s. She says it just isn't going to happen. But her husband pushes himself to try to keep up.

I now try to be kinder to myself. I spend at least one day a week at home, on my computer — planning jobs, doing accounts, or writing my books. I need the physical downtime. It's not always achievable, especially when I'm in the midst of a big job. But when I can, I build that rest time into my schedule.

On the plus side, plumbing has given me so much. I've had such a great adventure. I've met (and worked) with people whom I wouldn't otherwise have come across.

I've been to plumbing conferences and trade shows, I've looked around factories, I've been on countless specialist courses. And it's all been such a fantastic adventure.

I'm fascinated with plumbing. I've loved learning about boilers and heating systems. I really enjoyed the various plumbing and boiler courses I went on. But the learning continues. There's always something technical to read up on, or research. And I love that side of the job. Plumbers with more than 30 years of experience still say they are still learning new things each week. They say that 'every day is a school day'. It's impossible to know it all.

I also love the skills I have. At home, if something breaks, I'm more likely able to fix it. I'm not reliant on waiting for my husband to get around to it.

Recently, our electric shower broke. Within a week, I'd ordered a new one and had re-installed it. I declared it an 'emergency repair', because myself and my daughter love having showers. I discussed the repair with Rob and his parents over dinner.

"Oh yeah, the shower broke," I said. "I really like my showers. So I had to put a new one on the wall before I could shower again."

They all laughed.

"Do you know how weird that sounds?" asked Rob.

I saw his point. It's not a common thing for a wife to say. But these skills make me feel good. Being able to fix things makes me feel resourceful, and independent, and more in control of my life and surroundings. And plumbing has taught me so much more. On a personal level, I've discovered more about myself — both my strengths and weaknesses.

I'm finally starting to feel competent and confident. It's not how I thought it would feel. My confidence has grown enough to let me admit that I can't handle every job. I can admit that I don't know it all, and that I'm learning more every day. The more I learn, the more I realise I don't know — there are just so many scenarios and types of boiler/fire/etc out there.

There was once a time when I thought that being a plumber meant that I had to be able to do everything. But that's not realistic. For example, I don't unblock outside drains. So I forward those requests to a local specialist drainage engineer. Or for electrical issues, I suggest an electrician.

But otherwise, my approach is to give myself time to find out how to fix the issues (if I don't already know). It seems to work. I'm having success where previous plumbers have failed.

One of my new customers had previously been told their radiators were so chocked up with sludge that they'd need new radiators. Armed with a thermal camera, I discovered that the radiators were pretty clear. Later in the job, when I did a routine flush of the heating system, not much dirt came out. I saved them the cost of replacing their entire heating system.

Another customer wanted a new gas hob fitting. The previous installer had struggled to secure the front edge of the hob into the worktop. As a result, it would flip up slightly (if pulled). I saw the issue he'd faced. But with a bit of imagination (and my handy tools) I found a way around it. My customers were delighted. I was their 'golden girl'.

I also service a boiler every year in a local church/childcare centre. For the first year after installation, they'd struggled to get all the radiators hot. The original installers had failed to remedy the problem. Within moments of my first visit, I'd discovered the issue — their boiler had been set to a low setting within the programming. Once I adjusted it, the boiler flew into action, and all the radiators were beautifully hot.

But not every job is filled with such triumph. Most jobs are routine. And sometimes, I look at my work and feel I could have done better. I'm my own harshest critic. It's not enough for me to have a happy customer. I also need to be happy with my work. Sometimes I'm not. But that's inevitable.

And it's also sometimes inevitable that the customer isn't happy, and quite legitimately. Sometimes, I stuff up. Such as installing a square sink ever so slightly wonky (and having to later face the embarrassment of removing it and repositioning it), or drilling a hole in the wrong place on a tile — silly mistakes that I should have avoided. I have to face the issues, and sort them out.

This is all part of the learning curve. Many plumbing tutors warned me that I'd make mistakes. It couldn't be avoided. But it's still not nice to face them.

I want to be the kind of person who looks for better ways and solutions. I prefer to learn from other people's mistakes than my own. But either way, this is how experience is developed.

So what are my good and bad points? That might help me to figure out whether I would 'do it again'. On the plus side, I'm conscientious. And also tenacious. I'm able to problem-solve and find solutions.

Customers like me. I'm attentive, and I try to explain the issues to them. Women especially like me, having sometimes felt talked down to by previous (male) plumbers.

I'm also a great organiser. I use an online diary to schedule work. I'm good at organising various jobs, materials lists and booking electricians/other trades as needed. I keep on top of emails and phone calls, and my accounts.

But on the downside is anxiety. It never really goes away. Fifteen years into my plumbing career, and I still struggle with anxiety.

I don't like the uncertainty of not knowing what will crop up. Who will phone? What will they want? Will I be able to cope? Will I get a call saying one of my joints has burst and I've flooded a house? I have plumber friends who have received those calls. It happens.

I rarely answer my phone — I don't like to be put on the spot (aside form the fact I'm often driving, or got my hands full so can't answer it). I don't like hearing it ring, so I keep it on silent. But I regularly check for voicemails. I really like voicemail. It gives me a chance to hear what they want, and briefly reflect on it before I call them back.

Which brings me to another of my downfalls. I can

sometimes be a bit reactive. Sometimes, my initial impulse can be that a job is too difficult for me. I still doubt my abilities. There's still a sexist little voice in my head that tells me I don't know what I'm doing, and that I'm second-rate, because I'm female. It's difficult to shake that voice. But given a few minutes to think through a task or problem, I'm more likely to be on top of things.

As the business grows, post-lockdowns, I stop advertising. I can't handle all the jobs that are coming in. Work is still abundant from existing customers. I always seem to be too busy.

Coupled with my family responsibilities, housework, etc. I get really tired, stressed and anxious. Sunday mornings are typically when the stress shows. On that brief morning when I can stop for an hour or two, I feel the physical effects of the anxiety — generally a tightness in the muscles across my forehead, and tightness around my jaw. And — as mentioned before — I sometimes get 'energy crashes'.

When I'm really anxious, I'm easily overwhelmed. I want my life to slow down. I want a quiet environment, to help soothe my mind. But in a busy family house, it's often noisy and chaotic. Action films on the TV feel like a verbal and visual assault on my senses. I still sometimes struggle to cope. Sometimes Rob wonders if he should shoot me with a tranquiliser gun, to get me to slow down. But I do now have coping mechanisms — such as meditation and yoga — which help a lot. So I'm managing stress a lot better these days.

With such big pros and cons in the scale, I still can't answer the question. Would I do it again? It occurs to me that sometimes these questions can't be answered. We make the best choices we can at certain times of our lives. And from those choices, we evolve. Life changes directions, and takes us to new places.

For the moment, I'm happy on the tools. But if/when that changes, maybe I could pursue other avenues. Perhaps I could move into management, running a team of engineers/plumbers? Or combine my plumbing and writing skills? Maybe I could edit a plumbing magazine? Or write plumbing industry reports? Or even oversee websites and marketing for plumbing firms? I'm only limited by my imagination. I'm still only 50. There is so much more to come, and I have so much more to offer the plumbing industry.

Getting this far into my plumbing career has been tough. At times I wanted to give up. But when I look at what I achieved, I am so proud of myself. And that makes it all worthwhile.

THE END

Sources

Footnote 1. Construction News. Date: 18/03/22. https://www.constructionnews.co.uk/government/percentage-of-women-in-skilled-trades-shows-little-change-in-a-decade-18-03-2022/

Footnote 2. UK Parliament. Date: 19/04/24. https://committees.parliament.uk/committee/203/education-committee/news/200976/why-do-boys-lag-behind-girls-at-all-ages-of-education-mps-to-investigate/

Footnote 3. HESA. Date: 19/01/23. https://www.hesa.ac.uk/news/19-01-2023/sb265-higher-education-student-statistics/subjects

Footnote 4. A review published by Gas Safe magazine, page 4. https://www.gassaferegister.co.uk/media/2490/decade-review.pdf

Footnote 5. The Apprenticeship Guide. https://apprenticeshipguide.co.uk/more-women-and-ethnic-minorities-in-construction-apprenticeships-than-ever-before/

Footnote 6. Powered Now survey. https://www.powerednow.com/blog/international-womens-day-women-in-trade

Footnote 7. The Guardian newspaper. Date: 06/04/22. https://www.theguardian.com/world/2022/apr/06/uk-gender-pay-gap-women-paid-90p-for-1-earned-by-men

Footnote 8. Starling Bank. Survey on pocket money given to children. Date: 19/10/22. https://www.

starlingbank.com/news/gender-pay-gap-starts-early/

Footnote 9. ReviseSociology. Date: 13/02/23. https://revisesociology.com/2023/02/13/gender-and-subject-choice/?utm_content=cmp-true

Footnote 8. SecEd. Attainment: Closing The Gender Gap. Date: 19/04/17 https://www.sec-ed.co.uk/content/best-practice/attainment-closing-the-gender-gap/

Footnote 9. BBC television. Date: 16/08/17.No More Boys And Girls, Can Our Kids Go Gender Free. https://www.bbc.co.uk/mediacentre/proginfo/2017/33/no-more-boys-and-girls.

Footnote 10. NPJ. Gender Similarities in the Brain During Mathematics Development. Date: 08/09/19. https://www.nature.com/articles/s41539-019-0057-x

Footnote 11. Griffith University. PHD thesis by Dr Karen Struthers. Date: 2016. https://research-repository.griffith.edu.au/handle/10072/365458

Footnote 12. HEPI. New research on the stereotypes formed at a young age, their long-term impacts and what can be done to tackle them successfully. Date: 14/12/21. https://www.hepi.ac.uk/2021/12/14/new-research-on-the-stereotypes-formed-at-a-young-age-their-long-term-impacts-and-what-can-be-done-to-tackle-them-successfully/

Footnote 13. FT. Plan For Five Careers In A Lifetime. Helen Barrett. 05/09/17. https://www.ft.com/content/0151d2fe-868a-11e7-8bb1-5ba57d47eff7

Footnote 14. H&S Lifting Solutions Ltd. What Is The Maximum Weight A Person Can Lift At Work? No date. https://www.hands-lifting.co.uk/what-is-the-maximum-weight-a-person-can-lift-at-work/

Footnote 15. Springer Link. Gender differences in strength and muscle fibre characteristics. Date: March 1993. https://link.springer.com/article/10.1007/BF00235103

Footnote 16. Breakdown of male and female body weights. https://nidsun.org/what-does-your-total-body-weight-consists-of-andwhat-are-the-proportions-of-fat-muscles-connective-tissue-and-bones/

Footnote 17. Our World In Data. Human Height. Max Roser, Cameron Appel and Hannah Ritchie. Date: January 2024. https://ourworldindata.org/human-height#:~:text=Where%20are%20men%20much%20taller,3%%20to%20over%2012%

Footnote 18. Alexander Orthopaedic. Why Are Some Individuals More Flexible Than Others? Date: 22/09/23. https://alexanderorthopaedics.com/blog/why-are-some-individuals-more-flexible-than-others/

Footnote 19. The Guardian. Halluncations And No Sleep: Jasmin Paris On Her Historic Ultramarathon. Sean Ingle. Date: 25/03/24. https://www.theguardian.com/sport/2024/mar/25/jasmin-paris-interview-barkley-marathons-ultramarathon-history

Footnote 20. TUC . British Workers Putting IN Longest Hours IN The EU. Date: 17/04/ 19.https://www.tuc.org.uk/news/british-workers-putting-longest-hours-eu-tuc-analysis-finds

Footnote 21.The New York Times. Even Among Harvard Graduates Women Fall Short Of Their Work Expectations. Claire Cain Miller. Date: 28/11/14. https://www.nytimes.com/2014/11/30/upshot/even-among-harvard-graduates-women-fall-short-of-their-work-expectations.html

Footnote 22.The Daily Mail. Plumbers Secrets Leaked! Darren Boyle. Date: 16/09/17. https://www.dailymail.co.uk/news/article-4890536/Plumbers-charge-women-elderly-simple-jobs.html#:~:text=Plumbers are discriminating against people,cent more for simple jobs.&text=Plumbing supply company Anchor Pumps,mixer tap in a kitchen.

Footnote 23. Albert Einstein College Of Medicine. Why Diversity Matters. Date: July 2013. https://einsteinmed.edu/uploadedFiles/diversity/why-diversity-matters-catalyst.pdf

Footnote 24. The Guardian. Fund Manager Launches Scheme To Invest In Firms With Women On Top. David Teather. Date: 26/10/09. https://www.theguardian.com/business/2009/oct/26/investment-fund-women-executives

Footnote 25. PHAM News. 3/4 Of Plumbers Have Work-Related Mental Health Issues. Date: 13/05/23. https://www.phamnews.co.uk/3-4-of-plumbers-have-work-related-mental-health-issues/

Footnote 26. Institute for Fiscal Studies. Living Standards, Poverty And Inequality In The UK. Date: 25/07/24. https://ifs.org.uk/living-standards-poverty-and-inequality-uk

Footnote 27. Local Governemnt Assocation. Debate On Support For Single Parent Families. Date: 14/03/23. https://www.local.gov.uk/parliament/briefings-and-responses/debate-support-single-parent-families-house-commons-tuesday-14th

www.ingramcontent.com/pod-product-compliance
Lightning Source LLC
LaVergne TN
LVHW010101170826
845678LV00012B/2204

* 9 7 8 1 0 6 8 6 7 9 4 0 7 *